LIGHTHOUSES OF THE CAROLINAS

A Short History and Guide

Terrance Zepke

Pineapple Presss, Inc.
Sarasota, Florida

Inquiries should be addressed to:
Pineapple Press, Inc.
P.O. Box 3899
Sarasota, Florida 34230

www.pineapplepress.com

LIBRARY OF CONGRESS CATALOGING-IN-PUBLICATION
Zepke, Terrance
    Lighthouses of the Carolinas : A Short History and Guide / by Terrance Zepke—
1st ed.
        p.   cm.
    Includes bibliographical references and index.
    ISBN 1-56164-148-0 (alk. paper)
    1. Lighthouses—North Carolina. 2. Lighthouses—South Carolina. I. Title.
VK1024.N8Z46   1998
387.1'55'09756—dc21
                                                                              97-45042
                                                                              CIP

Design by Kirby J. Kiskadden
Printed and bound by Edwards Brothers, Lillington, North Carolina

First Edition
10   9   8   7   6   5   4   3

To my parents, whose love and support outshines any beacon light, and to Martin Coble, who took me to see my first lighthouse.

TABLE OF CONTENTS

ACKNOWLEDGMENTS

This book could not have been completed without the aid of many people who went out of their way to provide photographs, verify facts, and open doors leading to invaluable research. My deepest gratitude to a very special group of people, and my apologies to anyone I may have overlooked.

Hunting Island State Park, Cheryl Bergman
Oak Island Coast Guard, Exhiliaryman Chaney
Southport, State Port Pilot
NC Travel and Tourism, Bridget Maupin
Georgetown County Chamber of Commerce, Nikki Baird
NC Department of Archives & History, Steve Massengill
SC Department of Archives & History, Andy Chandler
Carolinian Library staff
Greenwood Development Company, Brett Borton
International Paper Realty Corporation of South Carolina, Paige Camp
ADM Corporation
Dare County Tourist Bureau, Rebecca Moore
Sarah McNeil
Cape Lookout National Seashore, Laurie Heupel and Karen Duggan
Outer Banks Chamber of Commerce
Old Baldy Foundation
Outer Banks History Center, Wynn Dough
Cape Romain Wildlife Refuge, Ruth Thompson
USCG Historian Office, Scott Price
National Maritime Initiative, Kevin Foster
Outer Banks Conservationists, Bill Parker
Melrose Corporation, Karen Cerrati
USCG Ft. Macon, Lt. Jeff Fulcher
USCG Hatteras Inlet Station, Hank Macchio
Cape Hatteras National Seashore, Andy Kling
Staff at National Archives at College Park, Maryland, and Washington, DC
SC State Park Service, Mike Walker
U.S. Lighthouse Society, Wayne Wheeler
and to my editor June Cussen, for having confidence in my abilities.

INTRODUCTION

Ever since man graduated from dugout canoes to vessels big enough to carry supplies and travel great distances, some form of light has been needed to warn mariners where the ocean meets the shoreline. In ancient times, this was accomplished with big signal fires. Later, burning coals were placed inside a metal container suspended on a pole. Much later came light towers. One of the earliest on record, and one of the most famous, was an ornate marble structure built by the Egyptians in 300 BCE. It was known as the Pharos of Alexandria and stood for over 450 years before toppling in an earthquake.

The first lighthouse in America was built in Boston in 1716. Just over fifty years later, the first beacon illuminated the Carolina coast. This was the Old Charleston Lighthouse on Morris Island, South Carolina. The lighthouse we see today is actually the second structure on that site, since the first was destroyed during the Civil War.

Like the Old Charleston Lighthouse, North Carolina's Bald Head Light Station, built in 1795, no longer exists. But its successor, the Bald Head Island Lighthouse, or "Old Baldy" as it is affectionately known, still looks much as it did when it was first lit in 1817.

Since 1767, many lights have been placed along the Carolinas' coast. Some were traditional conical caisson towers; some, lightships; and some, massive steel skeletons. "Screwpile" lighthouses, which looked like oversized gingerbread houses, were so called because of their anchoring (a screw-like flange was fastened to the bottom of the pile foundation and "screwed" into the substrate). Gigantic, Texas-type towers resemble the off-shore oil rigs found in Texas.

Today, there are eighteen light towers still standing, scattered along the coast of the Carolinas. Because of radar and sonar innovations, these beacons are no longer necessary, but when they were built, they were crucial to all marine traffic from freighters to fishing boats. Look at a map of the Carolinas' coastline and you can easily see why. The coast is pierced with narrow inlets, sounds, and rivers, and the channels are ever-shifting, making it difficult to determine where the deep water ends and the shallows and sand bars begin.

North Carolina's Cape Fear River is the only direct deepwater access between the Atlantic Ocean and the state's biggest port, Wilmington. The entire route is full of channels and sand bars, beginning with the dangerous Frying Pan Shoals. For that reason, Bald Head Island Lighthouse, Oak Island Lighthouse, Price Creek Lighthouse, and Frying Pan Light Tower were constructed.

The other North Carolina lighthouses are on the Outer Banks, a succession of skinny islands stretching roughly 175 miles from Virginia southward to Cape Lookout. Here, the warm northbound Gulf Stream mixes with the cool, southbound Labrador Current, producing intense fog and creating shoals. These waters have been nicknamed "Graveyard of the Atlantic," because over six hundred ships have sunk in this area.

South Carolina's coast is just as treacherous as North Carolina's. The Georgetown and Cape Romain lighthouses were built to help vessels maneuver the inlets and channels of Winyah Bay and the Santee River, respectively. The Cape Romain shoals extend nine miles, making the Cape Romain beacon's role doubly important.

The Charleston lighthouses were vital for leading ships into South Carolina's biggest harbor, Charleston. Hunting Island Lighthouse helped light the way from Charleston to the Hilton Head and Beaufort areas, where the last of the state's lights were placed.

Congress realized that in addition to auditors and other civil servants, experts were needed to take part in decisions such as design, construction, and placement of these towers. So, in 1852, the Lighthouse Board was set up, comprised mainly of engineers, Navy officers, and topographers. In 1910, this became the Bureau of Lighthouses, which President Franklin D. Roosevelt abolished in 1939 in favor of making all beacons, buoys, and piers part of the U.S. Coast Guard's responsibilities. Today, with the help of the National Park Service, the Coast Guard still oversees these sites.

President Grover Cleveland also had a hand in changing "lighthouse law" by requiring keepers to be qualified government employees. This was an improvement, since the positions had originally been political appointments, and the appointees usually had no expertise or long-term commitment.

Many people played an important role in the history of our lighthouses. The fifth Auditor of the Treasury, Stephen Pleasonton, was a bean counter who had little technical expertise regarding lighthouses. His only concern was to keep costs down. Thus it was over two decades after Augustin Fresnel, a French scientist and engineer, invented the Fresnel lens that U.S. lighthouses began using them. This lens, which you'll read more about later in the book, was designed to greatly increase a light's range, making lighthouses much more effective.

Each lighthouse in North and South Carolina enjoys a unique place in history. Cape Lookout Lighthouse became a prototype for many later lighthouses. Cape Hatteras is the tallest in America. The original Bald Head Island Lighthouse and Old Charleston Lighthouse were among the earliest constructed in America; the Oak Island and New Charleston lighthouses were among the last built. The New Charleston Lighthouse even has an elevator, and with its 28,000,000- candlepower lens, is one of the most powerful lights in the world.

The Carolinas' lighthouses have survived much more than inclement weather. The Old Charleston Lighthouse was one of only two lighthouses south of Delaware Bay that survived the Revolutionary War. All of the lighthouses were damaged by retreating Confederates during the Civil War so they couldn't be used by Union soldiers. During World War II, some were shelled by German submarines during the Battle of Torpedo Junction, when over one hundred ships were sunk off Diamond Shoals.

Vandals damaged many of the lighthouses that were abandoned after being decommissioned. Mother Nature has also done her part. Erosion has threatened nearly every lighthouse built in both states. Also, these coastal areas have always been especially vulnerable to hurricanes. In fact, progress on this book was impeded by a series of hurricanes in 1996, including Bertha, Eduard, Fran, and Hortense. After the storms pass, there is always serious discussion about whether homes and businesses in particularly vulnerable areas should be allowed to be rebuilt. This also raises the question of how much work should be done to (and money spent on) the lighthouses, since hurricanes and erosion will ultimately claim them.

I have lived most of my life in North and South Carolina, and while I have always enjoyed visiting our lighthouses, it wasn't until this project that I came to fully appreciate them and their place in history. This book reflects my feelings, and serves as both a historical summation and a guidebook. So I hope—whether you're a lighthouse enthusiast, historian, photographer, or tourist—you'll find this a useful, as well as inspiring, resource.

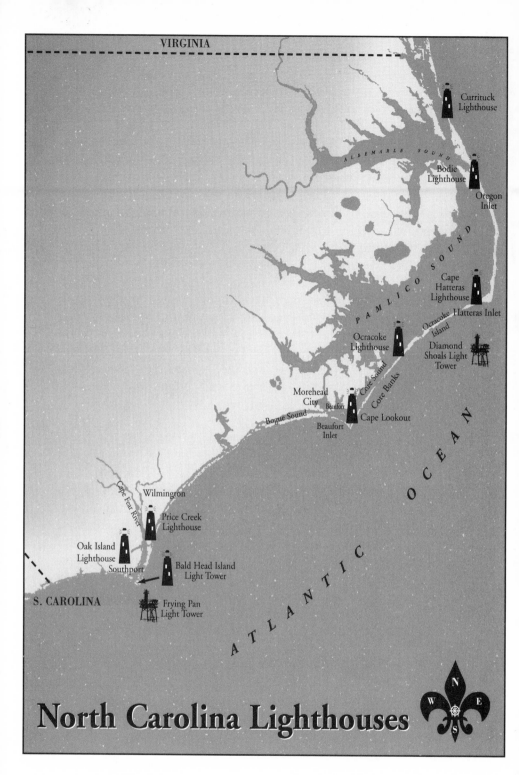

VIRGINIA

Currituck
Lighthouse

ALBEMARLE SOUND

Bodie
Lighthouse

Oregon
Inlet

PAMLICO SOUND

Cape
Hatteras
Lighthouse

Ocracoke   Hatteras Inlet
Island

Ocracoke
Lighthouse

Diamond
Shoals Light
Tower

Core Sound

Morehead
City

Cape Banks

Core Banks

Beaufort

Bogue Sound

Beaufort
Inlet

Cape Lookout

Cape Fear River

Wilmington

Price Creek
Lighthouse

Oak Island
Lighthouse

Southport

Bald Head Island
Light Tower

S. CAROLINA

Frying Pan
Light Tower

ATLANTIC OCEAN

ATLANTIC

North Carolina Lighthouses

N
W   E
S

LIGHTHOUSES
OF
NORTH CAROLINA

The ship was cheered, the harbor cleared,
Merrily did we drop
Below the kirk, below the hill,
Below the lighthouse top.

— Samuel Taylor Coleridge (1772-1834),
excerpted from *The Eolian Harp*

1795 — Bald Head Island
1802 — Cape Hatteras
1803 — Cape Hatteras lit
1812 — Cape Lookout
1817 — Bald Head rebuilt
1823 — Ocracoke
1848 — Bodie
1849 — Price Creek and Oak Island
1859 — Cape Lookout rebuilt
1859 — Bodie rebuilt
1870 — Cape Hatteras rebuilt
1872 — Bodie rebuilt
1875 — Currituck
1879 — Oak Island rebuilt
1958 — Oak Island rebuilt
1966 — Frying Pan
1967 — Diamond Shoals

CURRITUCK LIGHTHOUSE

Fast Facts

- Currituck Lighthouse was the last brick lighthouse built on the Outer Banks (1875).
- It cost $178,000 to complete.
- It stands 162 feet tall.

Built in 1875 and towering 162 feet over Currituck Beach is Currituck Lighthouse. Requiring one and a half years to build and several appropriations totaling $178,000, it was the last of four beacons placed at intervals from Cape Henry (Virginia) to Cape Hatteras. Currituck Lighthouse is located thirty-four miles south of Cape Henry Lighthouse, and thirty-two and a half miles north-northwest of Bodie Island Lighthouse.

An excerpt from an 1872 Annual Report by the Light-House Establishment to Congress emphasizes the necessity of a beacon along this stretch of coast:

> . . . the earnest attention of Congress (is) called to the importance of establishing this needful lighthouse. The distance from Body's Island [early spelling of Bodie Island] to Cape Henry is eighty miles, of which there is an unlighted space of forty miles. The land along the coast in this vicinity is low and in many places without trees, so even in day-time there is danger of vessels getting into unsafe proximity to the coast before becoming aware of it. The danger is enhanced by the fact that vessels bound around Cape Hatteras from the northern and eastern ports keep well to the westward, in order to avoid the strong current of the Gulf Stream, and for the additional reason

Currituck Lighthouse and close-up of U.S. Lifesaving Station, ca. 1889. Courtesy of National Archives.

they have a favorable current of about a mile an hour, nearly as far as Hatteras, and a smoother sea in bad weather; but in the absence of powerful sea-coast lights sufficiently near each other to give warning of approach to danger, many vessels laden with valuable lives and cargoes are in danger of being lost between these points.

The tower was actually approved, and Congress released funds for it in the 1860s, but the Civil War delayed construction. When the lighthouse was finished in 1875, it was nearly identical to Bodie Island Lighthouse.

In 1874, while the lighthouse was being built, a U.S. Lifesaving Station was also established at Currituck. The station was the first of many that were later placed along the Outer Banks.

Because Currituck Sound was (and is) very shallow, the big vessels that brought in the bricks and other building supplies had to anchor as far as eight miles out. Shallow-bottomed boats carried supplies the rest of the way. When supplies reached the dock, they

Fenced-in area of Currituck Lighthouse and keeper's house, U.S. Lifesaving Station, and outbuildings, ca. 1893-1899. Courtesy of North Carolina State Archives.

were then carried by a cart on the tramway, which extended from the wharf to the lighthouse site.

It took about a million red bricks to build the tower. It rises from a stone and timber piling foundation, which extends seven feet below ground. The base walls are five feet eight inches thick, decreasing to three feet at the parapet.

Since the four Outer Banks lighthouses so closely resembled one another, the Lighthouse Board ordered them painted with different patterns to make them easily distinguishable to mariners. Since the other lighthouses were already painted with black-and-white vertical, horizontal, and checkered patterns, the Board decided to leave Carrituck Lighthouse natural, probably to avoid the expense of repainting it from time to time. And so it remains today.

Aerial view of Currituck Lighthouse and Whalehead Club, ca. 1950s.
Courtesy of North Carolina State Archives.

Originally, the beacon was fueled by a mineral oil lamp with five concentric wicks, the largest of which was four inches in diameter. At a focal plane height of 158 feet, the light was fixed white, with a red flash. The flash occurred every ninety seconds, and had a five-second duration. The light was rotated by a clockwork mechanism beneath the lantern, which was powered by a line suspended by weights, somewhat like a grandfather's clock mechanism. The keeper was responsible for hand-cranking the weights every two and a half hours. During World War I, the three keepers also worked eight-hour shifts to keep a constant watch for enemy ships and submarines. The brick and iron sentinel still shines, serving as a valuable navigational aid.

In 1997, the lighthouse steps were reinforced with new stabilizing brackets. The first floor of the tower consists of a spacious hallway flanked by the original fuel storage room and the work room.

Keepers' duplex before restoration, 1979. Courtesy of Bill Parker.

Keepers' duplex during restoration, 1996. Courtesy of Bob Allen.

THE GREAT FRESNEL LENS

In 1819, French scientist and engineer Augustin Fresnel designed a lens that, combined with lamps and parabolic reflectors, provided optimum light for mariners. The lens consisted of prisms above and below the lighting apparatus (oil lamps and reflectors). The prisms magnified the lighting apparatus, but since they were not effective beyond a 45-degree angle, Fresnel put mirrors at the top of the lens as well. The entire system rotated on a pedestal.

Fresnel lenses advanced to different types and orders (or sizes) to better serve mariners. The three types still used today—fixed, flashing, and fixed-varied-with-flash—come in seven orders. The 1st, 2nd, and 3rd orders are the most powerful and are used in seacoast lighthouses. The 4th, 5th, and 6th orders are smaller and less powerful and are used for inland lights (e.g., sounds and inlets). The 3½ order lens was created by manufacturers who saw the need for an "in-between" order.

The following table shows the height of each order of Fresnel lens.

1st	7'10"
2nd	6'1"
3rd	4'8"
3½	3'8"
4th	2'4"
5th	1'8"
6th	1'5"

Visitors can walk along the black and white marble floor and then climb the 214 steel steps of the circular stairway to the gallery to see the top of the lens. If they could access the lantern room above, they'd be able to see the thousand-watt bulb, which is encased in a 1st-order Fresnel lens.

Automated in 1939, the electric light now has a flash pattern of three seconds on seventeen seconds off, and can be seen from almost nineteen miles out to sea. The lamp changer, an automated system of rotation and replacement of burned-out bulbs, also holds a back-up bulb. (Formerly, three back-up bulbs were used.) A generator provided electricity until grid electricity reached Corolla in the 1950s.

Currituck's 1st-order Fresnel lens, 1990. Courtesy of Debra Johnston.

Close-up of lens and lamp changer, 1990. Courtesy of Debra Johnston.

There are two keepers' houses. The smaller house was moved to the site, circa 1920, to accommodate a third keeper. It currently houses a museum shop, open seasonally, which sells lighthouse-related items. Some of the exhibits in the lighthouse itself include one of the white porcelain door escutcheons (plates that surround key-holes); replicas of a keeper's hat insignia, service badge and uniform buttons; numerous historical photographs; and old annual reports.

The larger residence, now in the process of being restored, was a prefabricated Victorian-style duplex that was built in 1876, transported to Currituck by barge, and assembled on-site. It is now listed on the National Register of Historic Places.

Restoration began in the early 1980s, at which time there were no windows or doors, the porches had collapsed, and vines grew inside and outside the house. In 1996, red cedar shingles were used to reroof the house, restoring it to the way it looked originally. The only difference between the new shingles and the old is that the new shingles are fire-retardant. The house is open only on special occasions due to ongoing renovations.

Major credit for the ongoing restoration and maintenance goes to the Outer Banks Conservationists (OBC), who lease all the buildings (excluding the lighthouse) and grounds from the State of North

Carolina. The tower is leased from the U.S. Coast Guard. OBC funds come from grants, donations, and the small fee that visitors pay to tour the tower and grounds. The OBC hopes to raise enough money to restore the larger house to its original state. Although the exterior restoration is mostly complete, interior work remains to be done. Plaster walls and pine floors have been repaired, and eventually the mantels and missing millwork will be replaced. Also, a storehouse/privy building on the grounds has been restored, along with two water cisterns. The cisterns were placed at each end of the keepers' duplex so that each keeper had his own water supply.

Directions: The lighthouse is in the town of Corolla and is generally open from Easter to Thanksgiving. Take NC 12 to Currituck Beach. Call 252-453-4939 for hours of operation for the lighthouse and museum shop.

Other Points of Interest

Kill Devil Hills Lifesaving Station. Transported from Kill Devil Hills to Corolla in 1986, this is now a shop. However, lifesaving memorabilia is housed next door at Twiddy & Co.

Directions: Located near lighthouse off NC 12, Corolla.

Currituck National Wildlife Refuge. The refuge comprises 1,800 acres filled with incredible species of birds and mammals such as blue heron, wild boar, and wild horses.

Directions: Take NC 12, north of Corolla, and follow signs to where paved highway ends at park entrance.

Whalehead Club. Once a sleepy fishing community, Currituck Beach remained undiscovered by developers until the mid-1970s. Today, this twenty-three-mile stretch of prime coastal terrain is lined with Beverly Hills-sized mansions, one of which is the Whalehead Club. This 20,000-square-foot mansion was built in 1925 by wealthy railroad industrialist Edward Collins Knight for his wife, who was refused admission to the all-male Lighthouse Club (a hunting club). Exorbitantly expensive, the Whalehead Club cost almost $385,000 to build in 1925.

Although the mansion has fifteen bedrooms, the Knights never entertained large numbers of people in the Gatsby tradition, as is often reported.

Whalehead is now owned by Currituck County. It is open seasonally to the public for a small fee, which is used for renovations, upkeep, and a future wildlife museum.

Directions: Whalehead is located near the lighthouse, facing the sound. For more information call 252-453-9040.

Useful Addresses and Resources

Dare County Tourist Bureau
P.O. Box 399
Manteo, NC 27954
1-800-446-6262
Covers Outer Banks from Currituck County, and stops at Hyde County (Ocracoke).

Outer Banks Chamber of Commerce
P.O. Box 1757
Kill Devil Hills, NC 27948
252-441-8144

Outer Banks Conservationists
P.O. Box 970
Manteo, NC 27954
252-473-5518
Memberships dues are nominal and include a certain number of free visits, as well as preservation updates.

BODIE ISLAND LIGHTHOUSE

Fast Facts

- Popular folklore says that the island got its name because of the many bodies found around it, washed up from shipwrecks.
- The first keeper of Bodie Island Lighthouse was paid an annual salary of $400.
- The tower still houses a 1st-order Fresnel lens.

The area this lighthouse serves is an isolated stretch thirty-five miles north of Cape Hatteras. Bodie Island is no longer an island, but a peninsula attached to Nags Head, Kitty Hawk, and Virginia Beach.

The brick light sentinel with alternating black-and-white painted bands that we see today is actually the third Bodie Island Lighthouse. Because Oregon Inlet continually shifts southward, the remains of the two original lighthouses have long since been washed away.

The first one sat on fifteen acres of land that the federal government had purchased for $150 in 1846. Two years later, the structure had been built and was lit. This first lighthouse stood fifty-four feet tall and measured seventeen feet around the widest part of its base. Close to the tower was a five-room house for the keeper, as well as a large brick cistern and two outbuildings.

Positioned just south of Oregon Inlet, Bodie's light was supposed to have a visibility of twelve miles. However, there were problems with the light from the very beginning. Over $2,300 had to be added to the amount originally allocated for the entire project—$8,750 (a tiny sum even in those days)—in order to install a

Photocopy of a diagram of Bodie Island keepers' duplex, ca. 1872. Courtesy of Outer Banks History Center and National Park Service, Cape Hatteras National Seashore.

lighting apparatus. The light consisted of a ten-foot lantern with fourteen individual revolving lamps and parabolic reflectors.

Additionally, there were structural shortcomings that prevented the light mechanism from ever working properly. The poorly-constructed foundation developed major cracks and leaks. Eventually it settled off-center and began to sink. The decision was made to rebuild rather than attempt to repair the tower's numerous problems.

The question of how a tower could be so badly designed and constructed deserves answering. At that time, the Fifth District Auditor of Treasury, the source who approved all lighthouse expenditures, was Stephen Pleasonton. Auditor Pleasonton guarded the government's money a little too thoroughly. First, he did not budget enough money for a proper foundation. Second, since he was more concerned about saving money than understanding the technical aspects of lighthouses, the cheaper lighting system he approved was inferior to the Fresnel system and never worked as it should have.

Lifesaving Station on Outer Banks, ca. 1900. Courtesy of North Carolina State Archives.

Only eleven years after the original Bodie Island Lighthouse was built, a second tower was completed. Since Stephen Pleasonton was no longer Auditor, the new lighthouse was designed by the Army Corps of Engineers. Additionally, when the second Bodie was completed, it was inspected to ensure that the proper building materials had indeed been used, and that the finished structure looked as it should.

The new lighthouse was a graceful, eighty-foot-tall, whitewashed brick structure. It was equipped with a 3rd-order Fresnel lens, which flashed every ninety seconds and could be seen from fifteen miles out to sea. All might have gone well if the Civil War had not started two years after the new lighthouse went into service. As the Confederates lost their hold on the Outer Banks, they retreated, but not before wreaking havoc on the lighthouse, which was close to a Confederate fort. They blew it up so approaching Union soldiers couldn't use it.

Because of the island's location, it was inevitable another Bodie Island Lighthouse would be constructed. In 1872, when the federal government allotted $140,000 to build a lighthouse, keepers' ac-

Bodie Island Lighthouse, ca. 1960s. Courtesy of North Carolina State Archives.

commodations, and several outbuildings, the third and current sentinel was erected. Construction was supervised by the same foreman who had been in charge of building the Cape Hatteras Lighthouse, Dexter Stetson. He used the same construction techniques that made the Hatteras foundation so solid, a sophisticated method of "stacking" timber pilings below the ground and placing granite blocks above the base. Located about one half mile from the ocean

Interior stairwell of Bodie Island Lighthouse, no date. Courtesy of Cape Hatteras National Seashore and Outer Banks History Center.

and just north of Oregon Inlet, Bodie now houses a 1st-order Fresnel lens, which lights a range of nineteen miles to sea.

This 150-foot lighthouse was originally a fixed light illuminated by a vapor lamp. A large container of kerosene oil was lugged every day from the oil shed into the tower, and then up its 214 steps to the lantern room. The lamp was filled, and the wick was cleaned, trimmed, and then lit. When electricity replaced oil in the early 1930s, the steady beam was replaced by a flashing light. The oil shed became home to a generator, although the smell of years of kerosene use can never be fully erased. In the 1950s, the lighting system was changed once again, becoming an automated 160,000-candlepower beam. Although the light is not really needed today as a navigational aid, it is comforting to see the beacon "come to life" each evening.

Bodie Island Lighthouse   17

The tubular-shaped tower is not open to the public, but the keepers' duplex is. The wall that separated the two keepers' quarters has been removed, and the former living area now serves as a visitor center. The center has exhibits, restrooms, and a gift shop, and has improved its collection of lighthouse and maritime displays. New exhibits were added in 1995 and include artifacts from other Outer Banks lighthouses, such as part of a 1st-order Fresnel lens once used in the Cape Hatteras Lighthouse.

The Coast Guard has turned over the grounds and all buildings except the lighthouse to the National Park Service. A nearby U.S. Lifesaving Station, erected in 1874, is now used by Park Service personnel serving this area of the Cape Hatteras National Seashore.

Directions: The lighthouse is located eight miles south of the US 158 and US 64 intersection, west of NC 12.

For Additional Information
Call the Visitor Center at 252-441-5711. For visitors coming by boat, there is a marina near the public ferry landing, just north of Oregon Inlet.

Other Points of Interest

Cape Hatteras National Seashore. The lighthouse is part of this 30,000-acre preserve. The area has lots of beaches and marshes, which can simply be enjoyed or explored at length. One such area, called Coquina Beach, offers swimming, bathing, and picnic facilities, as well as the *Laura A. Barnes* shipwreck display. Birdwatchers can delight in the abundance of birds and waterfowl.

Directions: See directions to Bodie Island Lighthouse above.

Wright Brothers Memorial. The December 17, 1903 flight, taken at Kitty Hawk, made North Carolina the "First in Flight" state. Erected in 1932 as a tribute to the Wright Brothers, the 4,500-ton monument is now being lit for the first time since World War II. Standing sixty-one feet high, the beacon's light is visible from roughly six miles away. Major restoration has been done.

Directions: The memorial is located off NC 12, approximately halfway between Corolla and Bodie Island.

For Additional Information
Outer Banks Chamber of Commerce
P.O. Box 1757
Colington Road and Mustian Street (off US 158)
Kill Devil Hills, NC 27948
252-441-8144

Chicamacomico Lifesaving Station. One of the first of many lifesaving stations later placed along the Outer Banks, this station and outbuildings are considered to be one of the most complete U.S. Lifesaving Service/Coast Guard Station complexes on the Atlantic. The original building, built in 1874, was turned into a boathouse when the new shingle-style station was built in 1911. Both are included in the large complex.

Directions: Part of the 30,318 acres which comprise Cape Hatteras National Seashore, the station is located on NC 12 in Rodanthe, about twenty-five miles south of Nags Head. NC 12 is reached from either US 64 or NC 158.

For Additional Information
Call 252-987-2401 or write Chicamacomico Historical Association at P.O. Box 5, Rodanthe, NC 27968.

Useful Addresses and Resources

Cape Hatteras National Seashore
Hatteras Island Visitor Center
Off NC 12 at Buxton
252-995-4474

Dare County Tourist Bureau (Outer Banks of NC)
P.O. Box 399
Manteo, NC 27954
1-800-446-6262

Outer Banks Chamber of Commerce
P.O. Box 1757
Colington Road and Mustian Street (off US 158)
Kill Devil Hills, NC 27948
252-441-8144

Superintendent
Cape Hatteras National Seashore
Route 1, Box 675
Manteo, NC 27954
252-473-2111

CAPE HATTERAS LIGHTHOUSE

Fast Facts

- Cape Hatteras is America's tallest lighthouse at 198 feet high.
- It took 1.25 million bricks to build the tower.
- Over 175,000 tourists visit the tower and climb its 257-step staircase every year.

Sitting on the edge of a narrow ribbon of sand, the Cape Hatteras Lighthouse is both a monument to the engineering prowess of mankind and a lesson in the futility of battling the sea.

Since the 1800s, a lighthouse at Cape Hatteras has marked the eastern tip of North Carolina's Outer Banks near Diamond Shoals, the formidable twelve-mile sandbar that lies just offshore.

Diamond Shoals is the meeting place of two great ocean currents: the cold southbound Labrador and the warm northbound Gulf Stream. What makes the area so dangerous is the shifting patterns of sand created where these ocean "rivers" meet. These ever-changing shoals are sometimes only a few feet deep.

Before Diamond Shoals was clearly marked, the first clue sailors had that they were near the sandbar was the sound of the surf. Of course, by then it was too late. To give sailors sufficient warning, a lighthouse would have to shine a beam that could be seen beyond the treacherous shoals.

Funds for the first lighthouse were released in 1793, but due to bad weather and illness among the crew who were building it, the structure wasn't finished until 1802. Additionally, the U.S. government bought property for the first tower, but the land reverted to its original owner when the government did not build within the contract period. And, because of difficulty finding a keeper, the beacon

Original Cape Hatteras Lighthouse, 1861. Courtesy of North Carolina State Archives.

wasn't lit until 1803. The original lighting system consisted of eighteen oil lamps with fourteen-inch reflectors, and the light could be seen from twelve miles out to sea.

But neither its height nor its lighting apparatus was sufficient to shine past the shoals, so between 1845 and 1854, a series of repairs, modifications, and additions was made to the lighthouse. Twice, additions were made to the octagonal tower, finally raising it to a height of 150 feet. The original iron-and-glass lantern room was ten feet in height and ten feet in diameter—much too small. A larger lantern room was added to accommodate the eight-by-six foot 1st-order Fresnel lens that was installed in 1854 as the last light modification.

Unfortunately, these were just the first of the problems that plagued Cape Hatteras Lighthouse. Mariners and local residents soon began complaining about the granite, sandstone, and iron tower's drab appearance. Birds, attracted by the light, often flew into the lantern-room glass and smashed it. The keeper was criticized for not doing his job properly. Occasionally fires resulted when keepers accidentally spilled lamp oil. And ships were still going down from

Sketch of original Cape Hatteras Lighthouse after it was painted and otherwise altered, ca. 1862. Courtesy of North Carolina State Archives.

lack of a strong light to guide them. And erosion began eating away at the island shore in front of the structure.

Attempts were made to rectify each problem. Piles of brush were stacked around the tower base to curb erosion, a common approach at that time. The lighthouse was painted: the upper half red and the lower white. The keepers' quarters were rebuilt, and inefficient keepers were replaced. In 1824, a Diamond Shoals Lightship was for the first time stationed nearby to serve as additional aid for mariners.

Unfortunately, the numerous modifications that had been made to the Cape Hatteras Lighthouse were still not enough to adequately light the Cape. But nothing further was done until after the Civil War. During the war, the lighthouse served as a lookout post. When the Confederates were finally driven back, they removed the lighting system before they left so the Union soldiers wouldn't be able to use the lighthouse.

After the Civil War, money was finally appropriated for a light-

Cape Hatteras Lifesaving Station, no date. Courtesy of North Carolina State Archives.

house that would do a better job of protecting mariners and shipping interests from shipwrecks. Work began in 1868 on a new beacon modeled after the light at Cape Lookout (see Chapter Six) that would be located about 600 feet further inland than the original lighthouse, thus better protecting it from erosion. Bricks and other supplies were brought in to the isolated island by barge, and a tram railway was built to haul materials to the construction site.

The new tower was designed to be a whopping 198 feet tall, comparable to a skyscraper, so it needed a substantial foundation to support it. But since the Outer Banks were (and are) comprised mostly of sand, water began seeping in as soon as the workers dug below sea level. Chief Engineer Dexter Stetson chose pine timbers as the base of the foundation in hopes that they wouldn't decay in sea water. After the timbers were laid, a series of granite slabs were placed on top of each other, like steps. The last of these were put above ground level, and the tower built on top. Remarkably, an excavation done in the 1960s showed that the foundation was still as solid as the day it was built.

Despite outbreaks of malaria among the building crew members and the loss of some construction materials in a shipwreck,

Sketch of room of Cape Hatteras keeper's house, 1862. Courtesy of North Carolina State Archives.

work continued at a rapid pace, and the $150,000 conical tower light, equipped with a 1st-order Fresnel lens, made its debut on December 18, 1870.

The octagonal base of brick and granite, which measures twenty-four feet by forty-five feet six inches, was left natural. The black-and-white barber-pole paint job, or "candystriping" as it is more commonly described, was added in 1873 to make the lighthouse more distinctive by day. Today, the flashing beacon is automated, but at the time Hatteras was built, the keeper had to wind weights suspended on heavy cables in order to rotate the thousand-prism lens.

By the 1920s, erosion had once again become a major problem. By 1936, the sea was lapping at the base of the tower, so the Coast Guard decided to build a frame tower further inland and to abandon the existing lighthouse. Its light was moved to the skeletal structure erected roughly one mile inland.

On May 15, 1936, the last keeper of Cape Hatteras Lighthouse, Unaka B. Jennette, had the duty of shutting down the tower. "Cap'n" Jennette, as he was affectionately called, had served as the head keeper of the beacon since 1919, and had raised his seven children

Hatteras Inlet Beacon, ca. 1890s, one of only two photos known to exist of this light. Courtesy of Outer Banks History Center and the National Park Service, Cape Hatteras National Seashore.

during his service at Cape Hatteras Lighthouse. His son, Rany, is currently employed by the National Park Service and delights visitors with tales of his childhood and remembrances of a bygone time.

The Coast Guard gave the old lighthouse and surrounding land to the National Park Service, which incorporated it into its newly

Cape Hatteras Lighthouse with keepers' quarters, outbuildings, and "mosquito farm," ca. 1893. Courtesy of Outer Banks History Center and the National Park Service, Cape Hatteras National Seashore. ("Mosquito farm" was the term applied to a pond formed by rain, overwash, or a combination of both.)

formed Cape Hatteras National Seashore. Men from the Works Projects Administration (WPA) and the Civilian Conservation Corps (CCC) were brought in to set up the park, and were put to work creating dunes, filling sandbags to line the shore, building jetties, and planting sea grass. Residents hoped these efforts would result in relighting the beacon, but that would have to wait. War once again came to the Outer Banks, and once again the Hatteras Lighthouse was used as a lookout post. German submarines sank close to eighty ships off the Outer Banks.

In 1948, since its light was still deemed necessary and also since studies indicated that erosion had been reversed, the Park Service leased the Cape Hatteras Lighthouse to the Coast Guard so operations could resume. The result was that the light was moved from the steel tower built in 1936 back to the lighthouse, and has beamed its light from there since (the steel tower was dismantled at this time). The original (1802) lighthouse was demolished in 1870, but the

Cape Hatteras Lighthouse, ca. 1900. Courtesy of North Carolina State Archives.

Cape Hatteras Lighthouse with remains of original structure seen nearby, 1963. Courtesy of Martin Coble.

ISLAND MIGRATION

With regard to the Outer Banks, the term "erosion" tells only half the story. Coastal geologists call the constant motion of the Outer Banks "island migration" or "island rollover." As the sea claims the eastern side of an island, the western side grows toward the mainland. For example, the first (1803) Cape Hatteras Lighthouse was built one mile from the shore: Its foundation is now under water. The current tower was originally 1500 feet from the shore; now it's only about 120 feet from shore.

THE PLIGHT OF HATTERAS INLET BEACON

The Hatteras Inlet Beacon was built in 1856 to complement Cape Hatteras Lighthouse. Local residents preferred taking a shortcut across Diamond Shoals and through Slue Channel to reach Hatteras Inlet. To find their way, they needed a light that was closer to ground level.

The little red open-framework structure, known as Hatteras Beacon, contained a 6th-order Fresnel lens. The lens enclosed a fixed white light that could be seen twenty-five feet above the sea. As with most of the southern coastal lights, Hatteras Beacon was extinguished during the Civil War. Although it suffered no war damage, no one seems to know what became of its lens and lighting apparatus. Due to hurricanes and big storms, the wood light structure was repeatedly moved and repaired. Unfortunately, it eventually succumbed to a hurricane, and there were no further attempts to maintain a beacon at the inlet.

foundation remained until the 1970s, when it was swept out to sea by erosion. Sadly, by the mid-1980s, erosion once again threatened the tower's granite and timber foundation. Heated discussions have been going on ever since then to decide upon a permanent solution.

One short-term solution has been to bulldoze massive amounts of sand in front of the lighthouse to diminish the pounding from the waves, but some of the sand washes away again during winter storms. Moving the tower has been suggested. This has been done with smaller lighthouses and could be the best way to preserve Hat-

Cape Hatteras Lighthouse, 1996. Terrance Zepke.

EROSION AT CAPE HATTERAS LIGHTHOUSE
1870–1996

1996 ——— 120 feet ——— Atlantic Ocean

1995 ——— 150 feet ——— Atlantic Ocean

1982 ——— 300 feet ——— Atlantic Ocean

1870 ——— 1/4 mile ——— Atlantic Ocean

Chicamacomico Lifesaving Station, 1995. Terrance Zepke.

teras in the long run. However, estimates for the job run as high as $10-12 million, and funds of that magnitude are not easily available. Also, many people argue that moving the lighthouse will weaken it and leave it vulnerable to hurricanes. Still others feel that once the lighthouse is moved, it will lose its historical significance.

Cape Hatteras National Seashore Superintendent Russ Berry has said that if a Category 4 hurricane were to hit, the beacon stands only a twenty percent chance of survival. Recently, five North Carolina State University professors thoroughly inspected the tower—noting the cracks on its walls—and the surrounding shoreline. They believe the 3,000-ton structure can sustain being moved the suggested 2,900 feet west-southwest of where it currently stands. Even some people who originally protested moving it are now in favor of such a project, in light of increased technology and better understanding of coastal storms. The United States has only a handful of companies with the equipment and capability to undertake such a tremendous task. One such firm was given roughly one million dollars in 1989 to study the feasibility of moving the tower, as well as doing some needed restoration.

But Congress still must allocate the $12 million or so the move will cost, and careful planning must be done. Spring of 1999 is projected as the earliest possible date for relocating the lighthouse. Until then, three-ton sandbags have been brought in to protect the tower's base. An additional jetty—designed by the Army Corps of Engineers to be removable—was proposed to help buy time until funds to move the lighthouse were raised. Unfortunately, the North Carolina Coastal Resources Management Commission rejected the jetty permit application, so the lighthouse must be moved soon if it is to be saved.

While the future seems questionable for the beacon, for now, Cape Hatteras Lighthouse is open to visitors during the summer months, and the National Park Service operates a museum, gift shop, and visitor center in the nearby former keepers' quarters.

Directions: Part of the 30,318 acres which comprise Cape Hatteras National Seashore, the lighthouse is located on NC 12 in Buxton, fifty miles south of Nags Head. NC 12 is reached from either US 64 or NC 158.

Other Points of Interest

Graveyard of the Atlantic Museum. Displays will include paraphernalia from over one thousand shipwrecks that have occurred along North Carolina's coast. Exhibits will include a log book from the Civil War that has descriptions of actual battles with blockade runners; old Coast Guard and Lifesaving Station uniforms and medals; and some artifacts from what historians believe was Blackbeard the Pirate's boat.

Directions: Located at Hatteras-Ocracoke Ferry Terminal and U.S. Coast Guard base.

For Additional Information
Call 252-986-2995.

NOTE: The museum is scheduled to open sometime in 1999.

Wright Brothers Memorial. The Wright Brothers' four flights made on December 17, 1903 at Kitty Hawk made North Carolina the "First in Flight" state. Erected in 1932 as a tribute to the Wright Brothers, the 4,500 ton monument is now being lit for the first time since World War II. Standing sixty-one feet high, the beacon's light is visible from roughly six miles away. Major restoration has been done. A nearby visitors' center houses exhibits, gift shops, and restroom facilities.

Directions: The Memorial is located off NC 12 and US 158, approximately halfway between Corolla and Bodie Island.

For Additional Information
Call Outer Banks Chamber of Commerce (see address and phone number under *Useful Addresses and Resources*).

Chicamacomico Lifesaving Station. This was one of the first of many lifesaving stations placed along the Outer Banks. This station and outbuildings are considered to be one of the most complete U.S. Lifesaving Service/Coast Guard Station complexes on the Atlantic Coast. The original building, built in 1874, was turned into a boathouse when the new shingle-style station was built in 1911. Both are included in the large complex.

Directions: Part of the 30,318 acres which comprise Cape Hatteras National Seashore, the station is located on NC 12 in Rodanthe, about twenty-five miles south of Nags Head. NC 12 is reached from either US 64 or NC 158.

For Additional Information
Call 252-987-2401 or write Chicamacomico Historical Association at P.O. Box 5, Rodanthe, NC 27968.

Useful Addresses and Resources

Cape Hatteras National Seashore
Hatteras Island Visitor Center
(Off NC 12 at Buxton)
252-995-4474

Dare County Tourist Bureau (Outer Banks of NC)
P.O. Box 399
Manteo, NC 27954
1-800-446-6262

Outer Banks Chamber of Commerce
P.O. Box 1757
Colington Road and Mustian Street (off US 158)
Kill Devil Hills, NC 27948
252-441-8144

Update on Cape Hatteras July 1999

The additional $9.8 million funding needed to move the endangered beacon was approved. The International Chimney Corporation of Buffalo, New York, and Expert House Movers spent from summer 1998 until April 1999 readying the lighthouse to be moved. Power was cut at the Cape Hatteras Light Station on March 1, 1999. In April, they began moving the Cape Hatteras Lighthouse to its new location, and the move was successfully completed during July 1999. By Memorial Day 2000, the lighthouse is expected to be fully operational and open to visitors.

DIAMOND SHOALS LIGHT TOWER

Fast Facts

- Diamond Shoals Light Tower was built in 1966 and automated in 1977.
- The tower is 175 feet high.
- It is equipped with a radio beacon, foghorn, and solar lighting system.

The Diamond Shoals Light Tower, built in 1966 to replace the Diamond Shoals Lightship, is one of seven East Coast offshore light stations. These light towers are often referred to as "Texas" towers, since they resemble the massive steel structures used in offshore oil drilling done in Texas. Only six Texas towers have ever been built, with two in North Carolina (Diamond Shoals and Frying Pan light towers).

Before the advent of sonar and radar, lightships supplemented lighthouses, providing added protection in particularly troublesome areas such as Cape Hatteras and Diamond Shoals. This area has been nicknamed "Graveyard of the Atlantic" because more ships have been lost here than anywhere else along North Carolina's coastline.

The first lightship at Cape Hatteras made its debut in 1824, but suffered irreparable damages during an 1827 storm. From 1827 until 1897, several lightships were moored here, only to break free from their moorings or to be hit by ships passing through the area. From 1897 to 1918, the next permanent lightship to be stationed here was finally sunk by a German submarine. The last lightship stayed until 1967 when the Diamond Shoals Light Tower was activated. The ship was then reassigned to Massachusetts and renamed the Boston Lightship.

Diamond Shoals Light Tower, ca. 1980s. Courtesy of North Carolina State Archives.

The Diamond Shoals Light Tower sits roughly twelve miles from Cape Hatteras, and the focal height of its lens is 125 feet. The light flashes white every ten seconds. The mammoth structure has a galley, eight bedrooms, and a communications center. A foghorn,

Close-ups of solarized lighting mechanism, March 1995. Courtesy of USCG Cape Hatteras.

radio beacon, and flashing light are part of the equipment found on the tower. The Diamond Shoals light can be seen from eighteen miles to sea.

The U.S. Coast Guard is responsible for the tower. Originally, it was run by a crew of eight or nine Coast Guard personnel, who worked two weeks on and two weeks off. But when the system was automated in 1977, personnel were no longer needed at the tower. Its automated system along with a radio signal indicate any problems to Coast Guard Group Cape Hatteras. Otherwise, the Coast Guard checks on it by helicopter once a year.

As with the Frying Pan Light Tower (see Chapter Ten), Diamond Shoals has a back-up system which will activate back-up lights and a signal to notify the Coast Guard Aids-to-Navigation Team if any equipment malfunctions. It is easily reached by helicopter if repair crews are needed. A maintenance crew, consisting of mechanics, electronics technicians, and electricians, used to work on the light station, but it became solarized (also as with the Frying Pan Light Tower) in 1994. Now the Coast Guard Aids-to-Navigation Team oversees repairs and maintenance. Since the lighting system was changed to solar power, the visibility decreased to only twelve miles: the light doesn't have as much candlepower as when it was run by diesel power.

View of Diamond Shoals Light Tower observation deck and housing for lighting apparatus, March 1995. This is also the helopad deck. Courtesy of USCG Cape Hatteras.

The future does not look good for Diamond Shoals Light Tower, which is already in poor condition. Hurricane Fran hit hard in 1996 and caused major damage, nearly destroying the structure, so it is now considered unsound. Maintenance crews, who used to stay on the tower one week at a time to maintain its generator, are no longer allowed to do so. Its windows have been smashed, the ocean supports are rusted, and the floors are almost rotted through. Its lower catwalks have been so beaten by waves that it is unsafe to approach by boat. A helopad at the Coast Guard Station Hatteras Inlet allows helicopters to land personnel, brought in from Elizabeth City, on the tower. However, the tower will probably be shut down for good in the near future. By the year 2004, the Coast Guard plans to decommission all Fifth District towers such as this one.

Although the tower is not open to the public, it can be seen from Cape Hatteras Lighthouse.

Directions: See Chapter Three for directions to Cape Hatteras Lighthouse.

OCRACOKE LIGHTHOUSE

Fast Facts

- Ocracoke, built in 1823, is the oldest North Carolina lighthouse still in continuous service.
- It is the second oldest lighthouse in the U.S. in continuous service.
- It is believed a fortified Indian village once existed at the site of this lighthouse.

Ocracoke Island is a sixteen-mile-long barrier island, located off North Carolina's Outer Banks and made famous by Blackbeard the Pirate, who used the tiny, uninhabited island as a hideout and hangout.

During Blackbeard's era, the colonists of nearby Bath saw the need to improve trade and navigation around this area of the coast. So in 1715 an act was passed to establish Ocracoke Island as a port. Local fishermen, who knew the waters well, became "lightering" pilots, guiding ships safely past the Ocracoke Inlet.

By 1730, more people began arriving on the island. Almost thirty-three years later, these squatters and their families were given twenty acres of land apiece. With the increase in population, colonists decided they needed a lighthouse to help vessels maneuver the inlet. However, many seamen felt a light should be placed at nearby Shell Castle Island instead. By 1790, a community was emerging on that island, and warehouses and even a tavern had been built for the lightering pilots.

Mariners preferred a lighthouse on Shell Castle Island to guide vessels safely through Ocracoke Inlet. Almost sixty merchants, sea captains, and other seamen signed a petition requesting a beacon be erected on Shell Castle Island.

Blackbeard the Pirate from Johnson's General History of the Pirates, *1724*

THE LEGEND OF BLACKBEARD

Ocracoke is a place where, legend says, a tall, dark stranger came to his gruesome death. His name was Edward Teach, better known as Blackbeard the Pirate. Born in 1690 to a wealthy British family, Teach was well-educated and quite handsome, with a muscular frame and thick, black beard. The story goes that he joined a group of Jamaica-bound sailors who were fighting Queen Anne's war against France in the early 1700s. He was hired as a privateer, a sailor sanctioned by the British government to rob enemy ships (provided they shared their haul with the monarch).

Teach fell in love with the pirate lifestyle and turned it into a lifetime career. After the war, Teach (as Blackbeard) stole a vessel for himself and began his own empire. By the time he moved to Ocracoke Island in 1718, he "owned" four ships and had four hundred pirates under his command. Although he loved women and tried to give up pirating for one of his fourteen wives, Mary Ormond (rumored to be his one great love), he could never abandon his ruthless lifestyle.

Not only Blackbeard's evil deeds—he once shot his trusted first mate in the knee just to remind his crew who was boss—but also the image he perpetuated made him so feared. Before attacking a vessel, he would tie fuses in his beard and set them on fire, creating a mystical smoke around his face to frighten his victims. After looting a ship, he and his crew would indulge in days-long parties.

Colonists on Ocracoke eventually tired of the pirate's intimidation and drunken partying and called on Virginia Governor Alexander Spotswood for help. Spotswood sent British Navy Lieutenant Robert Maynard with two ships, and in November 1718, Maynard attacked Blackbeard's sloop, *Adventure*, which was anchored in open water at Ocracoke Inlet.

Legend has it that it took five gunshot and twenty stab wounds to kill Blackbeard. The rest of his men surrendered or were killed in the skirmish. Legend also has it that Lt. Maynard took the pirate's head back to Virginia.

It is believed that the wreckage of Blackbeard's main ship, *Queen Anne's Revenge,* has been found near Fort Macon, North Carolina. But to this day, no one knows what happened to any of the treasure he must have hidden in the area.

Okracoke Lighthouse, February 1994. Courtesy of Dare County Tourist Bureau.

In the late 1700s, the North Carolina General Assembly passed an act to build Ocracoke Lighthouse. However, construction was delayed when in 1790 the federal government took control of all navigational aids away from the state government. And by this time, mariners had succeeded in putting a beacon at Shell Castle Island on land sold to the federal government by John Wallace and John

Historical aerial view of lighthouse and inlet, no date. Courtesy of North Carolina State Archives.

Ocracoke Lighthouse and keeper's house, ca. 1890. The two men and children posing in front of the house are probably the keeper, his assistant and their children. Courtesy of NC Archives and History.

Fresnel lens used in lighthouse, no date. Courtesy of Outer Banks History Center and Cape Hatteras National Seashore.

Gray Blount. It was approved in 1794, and finished and lit sometime between 1798 and 1803. Shell Castle Beacon was built by the same man who constructed the first Cape Hatteras Lighthouse (see Chapter Three), which partly explains the delays in finishing both lighthouses.

The pyramid-shaped wood tower was anchored in a stone foundation and stood fifty-four feet tall. The diameter of its tower was fifty feet at the base and twenty feet at the top. Its lantern held one huge, oil-fueled lamp.

For a while, the wooden lighthouse on Shell Castle Island played an important role in keeping mariners safe. But in 1818 it was destroyed by lightning. It was not rebuilt, since in the meantime the channel had shifted and the beacon had become useless. Shell Castle Island was abandoned soon afterwards. A $14,000 lightship was placed at Ocracoke Inlet in 1820, but it was also ineffective.

By the 1820s, Ocracoke Island had become a major shipping port, it was logical to once again consider putting a beacon on the island. Two acres near Silver Lake Harbor were purchased from

Shell Castle Lighthouse as seen on a Blount pitcher, no date. This is the only known recorded image of the wooden beacon. Courtesy of North Carolina State Archives.

Jacob Gaskill for $50. Approved in 1822, Ocracoke Lighthouse was lit in 1823. Built by Noah Porter of Massachusetts, the new lighthouse cost $11,359.35, including the three-room keeper's quarters.

The lighthouse stands sixty-five feet tall, rises seventy-five feet above sea level, and is made of brick covered with plaster. At the base, the walls are five feet thick. Originally, the squat tower was equipped with a flashing 3rd-order Fresnel lens, which was replaced

Shell Castle Lighthouse as seen on a Blount pitcher, no date. This photo shows more of how Shell Castle Island community looked. The lighthouse is detectable on the far right side of the pitcher. Courtesy of North Carolina State Archives.

with a 4th-order lens in 1854. Minor repairs were made to the tower and the keeper's house in 1855. The light and Fresnel lens were removed by the Confederates sometime during 1861 or 1862, so the Union couldn't use them. Both were replaced in 1864. Shortly after the war, the tower was repainted and numerous repairs were made. A second floor was added to the keeper's house, and in the early 1900s, a wooden walkway was built between the dwelling and the tower.

In 1946 the Ocracoke Lighthouse was automated and its keeper since 1929, "Cap'n" Joe Burrus, left its service. Cap'n Burrus, a lighthouse keeper for 45 years, also served at Cape Lookout Lighthouse and on the Diamond Shoals Lightship.

For a short time (1988-89), while the Coast Guard experimented with battery-operated rail lights, Ocracoke's lamp was not lit. But now the fixed white 8,000-candlepower light, which is visible from fourteen miles out to sea, comes on every evening before dusk.

In 1989, some minor repairs were made and painting was done. For safety reasons, the old wooden steps have been replaced with metal ones. The original four windows from the lighthouse were removed and almost destroyed, but were later restored, thanks to the Ocracoke Preservation Society.

The U.S. Coast Guard owns and oversees the lighthouse, since it is a working navigational aid, but the National Park Service maintains the lighthouse, grounds, and keeper's quarters. Funds to maintain the lighthouse come from federal grants such as the Bicentennial Fund. Attempts are currently being made to officially transfer Ocracoke Lighthouse and its outbuildings to the National Park Service. The Park Superintendent currently lives in the former keeper's house, which was last renovated in 1990.

Visitors are welcome to walk around the grounds and see the tower and outbuildings, but they are not open to the public.

Directions: Take NC 12, south of Cape Hatteras/Buxton to the ferry terminal. A free forty-minute automobile/passenger ferry from Cape Hatteras brings visitors in on the north end of the island, then it's a twelve-mile drive past marshland, sea oats and dunes into the heart of town.

There are also two toll ferries—Cedar Island (off US 70, north of Morehead City) and Swan Quarter (off US 264)—that arrive on the southern end of the island, which is also the heart of Ocracoke village where the lighthouse is situated. Each ferry ride is two-and-a-half hours long.

Call 1-800-BYFERRY for exact schedule and costs.

Other Points of Interest

Ocracoke Island. In 1990, the village of Ocracoke was placed on the National Register of Historic Places. The Historic District includes the lighthouse, Coast Guard Station, a British cemetery with the graves of Royal Navy sailors killed in 1942, and many historical buildings and homes. Capitalizing on its rich history and attractions, this former fishing community has over 600 permanent residents, many of whom own gift shops, bed-and-breakfast inns, lakeside cottages, seafood restaurants, and charter fishing companies. About 40,000 tourists visit this remote yet quaint island each year.

Visitors to the northern side of the island can see the "Banker" ponies, descendants of Spanish mustangs. (Debate is still ongoing as to how they got to the island.) At one time, the wild ponies roamed freely, but the Park Service fenced in about twenty acres to prevent the ponies from being hit by cars.

Also, the *Windfall,* a fifty-seven-foot gaff-rigged schooner that flies a skull-and-crossbones flag, offers evening cruises on Silver Lake and Pamlico Sound.

Visitors can also take a day excursion by private ferry to 250-acre Portsmouth Island on the northern tip of Core Banks (a fifteen- to twenty-minute ride). Once a thriving whaling village, it's now listed on the National Register of Historic Places. Many of the houses and buildings have been restored and make this former seaside town well worth a visit.

Directions: See directions to Ocracoke Island Lighthouse.

Useful Addresses and Resources

Dare County Tourist Bureau (Outer Banks of NC)
P.O. Box 399
Manteo, NC 27954
1-800-446-6262

Ocracoke Island Museum and Preservation Society
At Silver Lake, east of Park Service parking lot
252-928-7375

Ocracoke Island Visitors Center
Near Cedar Island & Swan Quarter ferry slips
252-928-4531

Outer Banks Chamber of Commerce
P.O. Box 1757
Colington Road and Mustian Street (off US 158)
Kill Devil Hills, NC 27948
252-441-8144

CAPE LOOKOUT LIGHTHOUSE

Fast Facts

- The present structure was built in 1859.
- The duplex of the former keeper's assistants is available to volunteer caretakers.
- The lighthouse played an important role in the Civil War.

Extending from the North Carolina coast 10 miles out into the Atlantic Ocean are the ever-shifting sands of Lookout Shoals. Many ships were wrecked on these shoals before a beacon existed.

Costing less than $21,000, the original Cape Lookout Lighthouse was authorized by Congress in 1804 and completed in 1812. Standing on a four-acre tract of land, the double-walled structure had an inside brick tower and an outside shell constructed of boarded and shingled wood painted with red and white horizontal stripes. The light was 96 feet high, and sat 104 feet above sea level.

By the 1850s, the sentinel had a list of problems. Sea captains complained the light was not bright enough, and severe cracks were appearing in the tower. Attempts were made to renovate the lighthouse, and plans were made to increase the tower height, but ultimately it was decided to build another one.

In 1857, Congress appropriated $45,000 to build a new lighthouse, and it was completed in 1859. Once finished, the circular red brick structure stood 163 feet above the water, and was equipped with a 1st-order Fresnel lens. This lighting system could be seen from approximately nineteen miles away. The assistant keepers' quarters were completed in 1873.

Lookout became the model for all lighthouses constructed on the Outer Banks from that point on. When all four Outer Banks lighthouses were finished (Cape Lookout, Cape Hatteras, Bodie, and Currituck), the Lighthouse Board painted each a different design so each was easily distinguished from the others and recognizable by daylight. For example, Cape Lookout's tower is painted with a black-and-white diamond-shaped pattern.

During the Civil War, the area surrounding the new Cape Lookout Lighthouse served as a military stronghold and a link in the supply line. When the Confederates were forced to retreat in 1861, they attempted to blow up both beacons so they would be inoperable for arriving Union soldiers. The original 1812 tower was almost completely destroyed, and the blast severely damaged the new lens and destroyed the wooden interior steps in the 1859 tower. But the following year, the Lighthouse Board relit the 1859 lighthouse with a 3rd-order Fresnel lens, which was used until the other lens could be repaired and reinstalled. In 1866, Congress authorized $20,000 to install iron stairs in and make minor repairs to this tower.

However, nature was exacting another toll on the new lighthouse and its usefulness. Waves breaking over the shoals often obstructed the tower's light. In 1904, a lightship was stationed at Cape Lookout to solve this problem.

The light was changed in 1914 from a fixed beacon to a flashing white light. The Coast Guard automated the light in 1950 and removed the Fresnel lens in 1975. The pedestal that once supported the Fresnel lens is now equipped with two thousand-watt aerobeams (airport beacons). The generator for an automated back-up system is located in the base of the beacon.

Lookout, like most other Outer Banks lighthouses, continues to suffer from major erosion. (Here it's sound-side, as opposed to ocean, erosion, caused by tidal currents in Bardens Inlet.) Very little shoreline exists to protect the lighthouse during storms. In 1979, a dredge reopened an old channel in Bardens Inlet. This action dramatically slowed erosion occurring near the lighthouse. Continued dredging operations throughout the 1980s and 1990s have kept this channel open and thereby reduced the risk to the lighthouse.

The tower was painted in 1985, and repairs were made to the unstable walkway and railing outside of the watch gallery. The keeper's house was moved farther down the island in 1950, and is currently a private residence. The assistants' duplex houses a small visitors' center and mini-museum on the first floor. The structures are listed on the National Register of Historic Places.

The U.S. Coast Guard owns and operates the lighthouse, and

Cape Lookout Lighthouse and keeper's house, no date. Courtesy of North Carolina Travel and Tourism.

Cape Lookout Lifesaving Station, no date. Courtesy of North Carolina State Archives.

the National Park Service owns the surrounding land. Personnel from the Fort Macon Coast Guard Station routinely check the rotating light by climbing five flights of stairs—197 steps—to a supply room that leads to the cupola. A steel door off of the supply room opens onto the watch gallery.

Cape Lookout's tower is closed to visitors. However, to get a good look at the lighthouse, visitors may take a small ferry from Beaufort or Harkers Island to the lighthouse or take their own boats. There are many launching sites for private boats throughout Carteret County.

If you crave a unique experience and some peace and quiet, the assistant keepers' duplex has been remodeled, and basic accommodations upstairs are available to volunteer caretakers for three-month stints. Duties include welcoming tourists, answering questions, and keeping the house and surrounding beach area clean. The house has electricity from the mainland.

The lighthouse is part of Cape Lookout National Seashore, a string of fifty-five miles of southern barrier islands ranging from the Beaufort Inlet to Ocracoke. The Shackleford and Core Banks comprise

Cape Lookout Lighthouse with outbuildings, keeper's house, and duplex of keeper's assistants, no date. Courtesy of North Carolina State Archives.

the land mass of Cape Lookout National Seashore. When visiting any of the sites of Cape Lookout National Seashore (see *Other Points of Interest*), visitors should remember that there are no facilities, and a hat, shoes, sunscreen, and insect repellent should be worn.

Directions: US 70 through Morehead City and Beaufort (twenty miles east) will take you right onto Harkers Island. Follow Harkers Island Road until it dead-ends at eastern end of island. On the left is the visitors' center (which offers an audiovisual presentation, exhibits, a gift shop, and restrooms). Signs are well-posted.

NOTE: Harkers Island is also a good place to see Cape Lookout Lighthouse without hiring a boat.

NOTE: There are several other boat launches or ferry points available, including Morehead City and Beaufort.

Other Points of Interest

The Cape Lookout National Seashore. The shoreline has many interesting sites including Shackleford Banks, the former fishing community once known as Diamond City. Shackleford has an old cemetery, and the foundations and remnants of former homes. With some time and effort, you can spot wild ponies anywhere from the shore's dunes to the thickest vegetation in the heart of the island. Cape Lookout is also a nesting area for the threatened loggerhead and green turtles. Core Banks is known for great fishing and shelling.

Cape Lookout Lifesaving Station. Established in 1887, this station is listed on the National Register of Historic Places as "Cape Lookout Coast Guard Station." The station was decommissioned in 1982.

NOTE: No public access to the Lifesaving Station.

For additional information
Cape Lookout National Seashore
131 Charles St.
Harkers Island, NC 28531
252-728-2250

The North Carolina Maritime Museum. This museum houses displays and exhibits of North Carolina's coastal history, including ship models. Visitors can browse on their own or take a tour that concludes at the museum's gift shop. The museum also offers educational excursions to nearby barrier islands and forests.

Directions: Take US 70 through Morehead City to Beaufort. Signs are well-posted, and the museum is located on a main street.

For additional information
North Carolina Maritime Museum
315 Front St.
Beaufort, NC
252-728-7317
No admission charge.

Useful Addresses and Resources

Cape Lookout National Seashore
131 Charles St.
Harkers Island, NC 28531
252-728-2250

Carteret County Tourism
(covers Harkers Island, Morehead City, Beaufort, Atlantic
Beach, and Emerald Isle)
P.O. Box 28557
Morehead City, NC 28557
252-726-8148

Concession or Private Ferry Services
Since ferry companies change seasonally, contact Cape Lookout
National Seashore for a current list of ferry services.

PRICE CREEK LIGHTHOUSE

Fast Facts

- Price Creek Lighthouse was built in 1849, the last of a series of North Carolina's inlet lights that were built along the Cape Fear River.
- One of the two original beacons was destroyed by a storm.
- The lighthouse is named for Price Creek, which rises in southeast Brunswick County and flows east into the Cape Fear River.

The last inlet light to be placed along the Cape Fear River was the Price Creek Lighthouse, which was built in 1849. Two structures were actually built on the river, and were part of a larger group of river lights that helped ships reach Wilmington, North Carolina's largest port. The lights included Oak Island, Campbell Island, Orton's Point, and a lightship at Horse Show. The beacons were configured as range lights that would line up to better reveal the inlet and help vessels navigate the channel.

The need for the lights first became apparent in 1761, when a hurricane created the New Inlet. The 1849 light, which had a range of thirty-five feet above sea level, was a basic wooden tower built on top of the keeper's brick house. The house was used during the Civil War as a Confederate States signal station, and was one of the means of communication between Fisher and Caswell forts.

Between the late 1800s and early 1900s, storms seriously damaged the house and tower. Eventually, they disintegrated, and local residents hauled away the rubble of bricks. I was told by the publisher of the local newspaper, the *State Port Pilot,* that there is a

Price Creek Lighthouse, 1996. Terrance Zepke.

Sketch showing how keeper's house with tower on top must have looked, no date. Courtesy of State Port Pilot.

house on Southport's Atlantic Avenue that was constructed with many of these bricks.

The second beacon was a twenty-foot circular brick structure whose light was twenty-five feet above sea level. It had a base diameter of seventeen feet, with walls that were three feet thick. The top measured nine feet across and had walls two feet thick. There was a window and a circular platform holding the framework for the lights. When the tower's height was raised about six feet, the platform was converted from circular to square.

The second tower was damaged during the Civil War, but never repaired. A seawall had to be built in 1881 to save the Wilmington harbor. This eliminated river traffic along this stretch of Cape Fear River, so there was no need to replace any of the area lights that had been damaged or destroyed during the war. Price Creek Lighthouse is the only one of these early river lights that still exists.

The structure's windows have long been missing, and the lantern room has been removed and the hole from its void boarded

Price Creek keeper's house as it looked after a storm damaged it, no date. Courtesy of North Carolina Department of Archives and History.

up. Today, the beacon remains in fairly good condition, considering that it suffered shell damage during the Civil War and has been abandoned for nearly a century.

Directions: Because it is privately owned by the ADM Corporation, there is no good way to see Price Creek Lighthouse close up. It can be seen from a distance on the Southport/Fort Fisher auto ferry (call 1-800-BYFERRY). The state ferry terminal is at Southport on East Moore Street. It is easy to find as signs are plentiful.

NOTE: Standing on the waterfront in Southport, you can easily see Oak Island Lighthouse to the right. In the distance is "Old Baldy" Lighthouse across the water on Bald Head Island.

Other Points of Interest

The Southport Maritime Museum. This museum houses nautical memorabilia of Lower Cape Fear. Take a self-guided tour or ask for a knowledgeable guide (nominal fee).

*Price Creek Lighthouse with girls posing on attached ladder, ca. 1960s.
Courtesy of North Carolina Department of Archives and History.*

For Additional Information
Southport Maritime Museum
116 N. Howe St.
P.O. Box 11101
Southport, NC 28461
910-457-0003

Useful Addresses and Resources

Southport Chamber of Commerce
4841 Long Beach Road SE
Southport, NC 28461
910-457-6964

OAK ISLAND LIGHTHOUSE

Fast Facts

- The present structure was built in 1958.
- Oak Island was one of the last lighthouses built in America and the last manually operated one in the world.
- Paint mixed into the concrete keeps the tower from ever needing repainting.

Uncertainty shrouds the history of the early Oak Island Range Lights. It is clearly recorded that two range lights were approved as part of a series of navigational aids that were being placed in the Cape Fear area. Oak Island was a logical choice for the lights, since it sits on the west side of the river mouth, "kissin' kin" to Bald Head Island.

The lighthouses were built to alleviate the dangers brought on by a growing amount of river traffic. The increasing numbers of boats and ships were the result of the formation of the New Inlet, which was carved out by a hurricane in 1761. The new route became the best way to reach the state's biggest port, Wilmington.

On September 7, 1849, these Oak Island lights were completed. Unfortunately, very little recorded information exists to detail these lights. The other Cape Fear River range lights — Price Creek, Campbell Island, and Orton's Point — were designed the same way, with one of the towers built atop the keeper's dwelling and a second, lower light built nearby. Oak Island is the exception to this string of river lights. It had two free-standing beacons and a separate structure for the keeper. All that is known with any certainty is what is shown in an 1859 U.S. Light List, which describes Oak Island Light Station as having two brick towers and a one-and-a-half-story

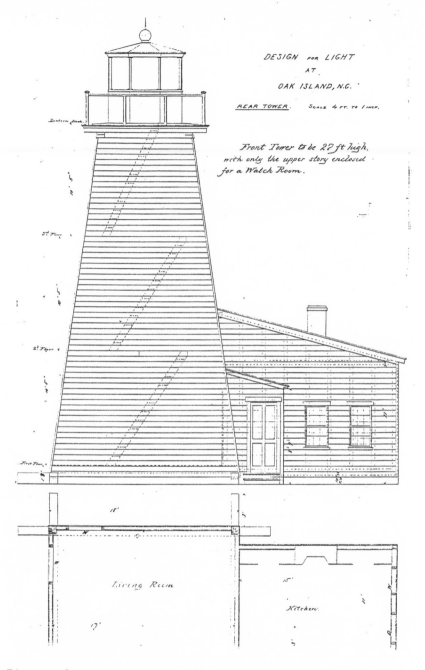

DESIGN FOR LIGHT
AT
OAK ISLAND, N.C.

REAR TOWER. SCALE 4 FT. TO 1 INCH.

Front Tower to be 27 ft high.
with only the upper story enclosed
for a Watch Room.

Diagram of a tower with living area and attached kitchen, October 20,
1865. Courtesy of National Archives.

64 Lighthouses of North Carolina

Oak Island Range Light Station, May 1, 1893. Courtesy of National Archives.

U.S. Coast Guard Station, Southport, no date. Courtesy of North Carolina State Archives.

Oak Island Coast Guard Lifesaving Station, Southport, no date. Courtesy of North Carolina State Archives.

Oak Island Coast Guard Lifesaving Crew, Southport, no date. Courtesy of North Carolina State Archives.

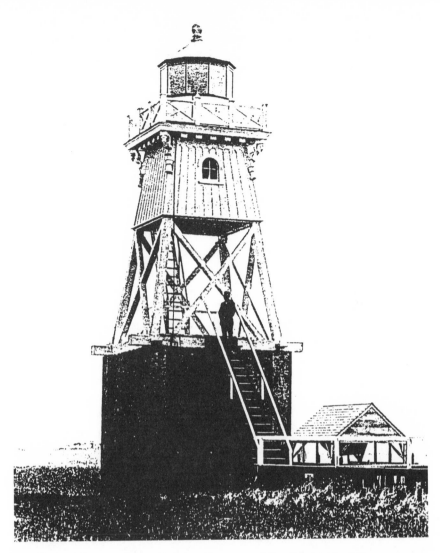

Oak Island Range Light, no date. Courtesy of Southport Maritime Museum.

keeper's house. This half, or "jump," story built above the main level was for sleeping space. The dwelling had a kitchen and porch attached to it.

These brick beacons were destroyed during the Civil War. Plans drawn in 1865, obtained from the National Archives, show a sophisticated rear Oak Island Range Light with four levels: living level; sleeping quarters; oil and store room level; and a watch tower at the top. A kitchen is attached on the ground or living level. The plans also indicate the front beacon would beam a light twenty-seven feet above sea level, and only its upper story would be enclosed (for a watch room).

For some reason, these plans were never used or at least extremely modified. A National Archive photo dated May 1, 1893, shows a very different, two-story keeper's house. Also, written records clearly describe the lights that were rebuilt in 1879: The front range light was a wooden structure with gingerbread-house elements, secured to a sixteen-foot high by fourteen-foot wide brick foundation. The foundation still stands today. The lower or rear light was a simple one, mounted on skids so it could be moved when the channel periodically shifted. What also lends to the confusion surrounding the Oak Island 1849 and 1879 range lights is they were commonly called the Caswell Lights, because of their close proximity to Fort Caswell.

Both 1879 range lights survived until 1893, when a hurricane did serious damage to the keeper's house and front beacon. The front beacon was rebuilt, although by this time the lights were no longer of any real importance since shipping routes had changed, no longer bringing vessels along this part of the Cape Fear River.

The following year, use of this light station was discontinued. Records do not indicate what happened to the rear beacon, but the front beacon was supposedly destroyed by fire. However, "Cap'n" James Henry "Sonny" Dosher, former keeper of Bald Head Island Lighthouse, has two great-granddaughters in Southport who are sure the wooden portion of the gingerbread-style beacon was sold many years ago at an auction for approximately $20.

Soon after the beacons were decommissioned, Congress approved funds for the much-needed Cape Fear Lighthouse. Located on adjacent Bald Head Island, the skeletal tower was finished in 1903 and replaced the antiquated range light. The new structure did its job well until a modern, more accessible lighthouse was built on Oak Island.

The former keeper for Cape Fear Lighthouse, "Cap'n" Charles Swann, threw the switch that activated the Oak Island Lighthouse on May 15, 1958. This was the last lighthouse built in North Carolina, and one of the last built in the United States. It stands an impressive 169 feet high, and is made of eight-inch-thick reinforced concrete. The black and white paint that gives it its distinctive markings was mixed with the concrete, so the structure would

Metal ladder leading to lantern room, 1996. Terrance Zepke.

never need repainting. The base was anchored 70 feet below ground to make it strong enough to support the tower.

Two Marine Corps helicopters were needed to put the lamp into place. The tower houses four thousand-watt aerobeam lights, which

Fresnel lens (1st-order) on display at Coast Guard Station, Oak Island, 1996. Terrance Zepke.

Close-up of lighting apparatus and aerobeams of Oak Island Lighthouse, 1996. Terrance Zepke.

Oak Island Lighthouse with helicopter lifting crown into place, ca. 1958. Courtesy of North Carolina State Archives.

flash intermittently and can be seen from twenty-four miles out to sea. With 2,500,000 candlepower, Oak Island is one of the most powerful lighthouses in the world. As a matter of fact, the light shines so brightly that black panels have been placed over the lantern room windows to prevent "spotlighting" the surrounding homes.

A shaft with a pulley to which a metal box is attached is visible upon entering the sixteen-foot-diameter base. This is used to haul tools, lamps, and other necessities to the top of the tower. To get to the platform, lightkeepers must climb the steep, narrow metal steps located to the left of the shaft. The keeper reaches the lantern room by a fourteen-rung metal ladder. This room is so crowded with the four huge revolving lights that it is almost impossible to enter the room while the lights are working without risking serious injury.

Oak Island is the last manually-operated lighthouse in the world. It is switched on each evening from the base of the tower at thirty minutes before sunset, and switched off each morning at thirty minutes past sunrise. An automatic back-up system takes burned-out bulbs out of rotation and replaces them with new bulbs.

The Coast Guard oversees the light tower. One person climbs the 134 steps weekly to inspect the lights.

The lighthouse is not open to the public, since it is on Coast Guard property, but visitors can easily see it from Caswell Beach.

Directions: Take NC 133 from Southport to Caswell Beach. When the highway ends, the road curves to the left. The lighthouse is about three miles from the bridge that connects this outer strip of coast to the mainland.

NOTE: The lighthouse is in a Coast Guard compound, surrounded by a chain-link fence. It can easily be seen from the road, which is only a few feet from the tower, or from across the street at Caswell Beach. It can also be seen from the waterfront at Southport.

Other Points of Interest

The Southport Maritime Museum. This museum houses nautical memorabilia of Lower Cape Fear. Take a self-guided tour or ask for a knowledgeable guide (nominal fee).

Southport Maritime Museum
116 N. Howe St.
P.O. Box 11101
Southport, NC 28461
910-457-0003

Useful Addresses and Resources

Southport Chamber of Commerce
4841 Long Beach Road SE
Southport, NC 28461
910-457-6964

BALD HEAD ISLAND LIGHTHOUSE

Fast Facts

- When it was built in 1817, Old Baldy cost just under $16,000.
- The octagonal tower is 109 feet tall, made of brick and coated with cement.
- The architect was Johnson & Sons of Goldsboro, North Carolina.

Part of Smith Island, fourteen-mile-long Bald Head Island got its nickname from the dunes on its south beach. River pilots used to stand on these dunes watching for ships that needed help to get safely up the river. Eventually, the dunes became so worn down, they looked like a bald head.

It made great sense to put a lighthouse here, not only to guide ships entering the labyrinth of channels and sand bars of the Cape Fear River, but also to help vessels avoid the treacherous Frying Pan Shoals, which reach over twenty miles into the ocean.

The Bald Head Island Light Station was North Carolina's first lighthouse structure, completed and lit in 1795. Unfortunately, the original structure was built too close to the river, and very soon a serious erosion problem developed. By 1810, a jetty consisting of a couple of rows of poles with brush piles in between, was put in place around the light station to shield it from further deterioration. Just three years later, however, the beach underneath the beacon began to erode, and the Collector of Customs in Wilmington announced that the structure would have to be torn down.

That same year, funds for a new lighthouse were approved, but it wasn't until 1816 that efforts really got underway to obtain

Bald Head Island Lighthouse, 1996. Terrance Zepke.

construction bids. The new octagonal tower, "Old Baldy," as it is now affectionately known, was first illuminated in 1817. At its base, Old Baldy is thirty-six feet wide and its walls are five feet thick; at its top, it is fourteen and a half feet wide and its walls are two feet thick. The foundation and the platform for the lantern room are stone; the

Sketch of the original Bald Head Light Station, 1805. Courtesy of North Carolina State Archives.

tower is brick, plastered on the outside. (Some of these bricks re-portedly came from the original Bald Head Light Station.) The ground floor is also of brick; the other floors, stairs, and joists are Carolina yellow pine. The original twelve-by-fourteen-inch double-glazed window panes came from Boston.

Because it was only ninety feet high and its 4th-order Fresnel lens had a very limited range, the structure proved unhelpful in as-sisting vessels past the perilous Frying Pan Shoals. In 1851, the Lighthouse Board asked for money from the federal government to raise the tower to 150 feet and to upgrade the lens to a 1st-order Fresnel. Instead of approving this request, Congress ordered a light-ship to be placed at Frying Pan Shoals. The vessel served as a navi-gational aid from 1854 until 1964, when its vulnerability to storms and hurricanes was deemed too great. However, the Lighthouse Board did change Old Baldy's lens to a 3rd-order and placed a fog bell near the tower in 1855.

Meanwhile, a new inlet opened up for the Cape Fear River sev-eral miles away at Fort Fisher, which meant there was no longer any great need for Old Baldy. It was decided that a tower should be built closer to this inlet. So in 1866, a framed structure with a watchtower on top was erected at Federal Point.

Shortly afterwards, the Confederates closed both towers to pre-vent Union soldiers from using them. After the Civil War, only the Federal Point Lighthouse was relit. A hurricane deepened the New

Federal Point Lighthouse, 1866. Discontinued ca. 1879. Destroyed by fire 1881. Courtesy of National Archives.

Inlet too much, and to save Wilmington's harbor a giant seawall, known as The Rocks, had to be constructed in 1881 to close the inlet. Now Federal Point Light Tower became ineffective, meaning that once again Bald Head Lighthouse filled a void. Ironically, this was also the year a fire destroyed the lighthouse at Federal Point.

When Old Baldy was reactivated, the 3rd-order Fresnel lens was replaced with a 4th-order lens. This meant it no longer qualified as a sea light, rather as a harbor light. A 150-foot stone jetty was built to thwart erosion, along with a large two-story house in 1883 for the keeper and his family. Due to the increasing water created by the inlet closing, another fifty feet was later added to the jetty to provide extra protection for the lighthouse.

Frying Pan Lightship, 1972. Courtesy of North Carolina State Archives.

Despite the combination of the lightship and Bald Head Island Lighthouse, sailors still complained of insufficient light for the treacherous Frying Pan Shoals. Again, the Lighthouse Board pleaded with Congress for funds to increase Baldy's height to 150 feet and to change the lens to a 1st-order Fresnel. These requests were denied. Instead, Congress approved a new beacon to be built at the highest point of Cape Fear to serve the growing number of ships en route to Wilmington.

In 1889, the Lighthouse Board finally accepted that Congress would not make improvements to Old Baldy and that a new beacon would be built instead. So the Board requested that the new structure be a heavy masonry tower. After this proposal was ignored for years by Congress, it was modified to encompass a wrought-iron-and-steel frame tower that would cost less than half what the stone structure would have cost. This plan was approved in 1898.

Nevertheless, it was 1903 before the $70,000 skeletal tower, called the Cape Fear Lighthouse, began its vigil. The necessity to build a pier and a tramway for hauling construction supplies caused the delay. To construct a tram meant cutting through thick vegetation before any track could be laid. Once finished, the tram carried building materials and supplies over the four-mile distance from shore to site in an iron-wheeled flat car pulled by a team of mules.

Aerial view of Bald Head Island Lighthouse, Southern Architect, *September 1963. Courtesy of North Carolina State Archives.*

The new lighthouse was two and a half miles from the old Federal Point light structure, much closer to Frying Pan Shoals. When finished, it stood 150 feet tall and had a 1st-order Fresnel lens with a range of almost nineteen miles. The lower part of the steel tower was painted white and its upper part later painted black. Stairs to the top of the tower and its watch room were located in the

Captain "Sonny" Dosher, long-time Bald Head keeper, standing in tower doorway, no date. Courtesy of Sarah McNeil.

Cape Fear Lighthouse, ca. 1906. Courtesy of North Carolina State Archives.

inner tower of the structure. The lantern room contained a 160,000-candlepower light, measuring a substantial ten feet in height and six feet in diameter.

The Cape Fear Lighthouse was decommissioned in 1958 when the modern Oak Island Lighthouse became operational. Sixty-two

Bodie Island Lighthouse with oil shed, 1995. Terrance Zepke.

Morris Island Lighthouse, 1996. Terrance Zepke.

Currituck Lighthouse as it looks today. Courtesy of North Carolina Travel and Tourism Division.

Price Creek Lighthouse showing water and tower, 1996. Terrance Zepke.

Former keeper's house at Sullivan's Island. Restored and currently used by Coast Guard personnel, 1996. Terrance Zepke.

C3

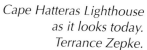

Aerial view of lighthouse and Ocracoke Inlet, February 1994. Courtesy of Dare County Tourist Bureau.

Close-up of lighting apparatus and aerobeams of Oak Island Lighthouse, 1996. Terrance Zepke.

Aerial view of Oak Island Lighthouse and Coast Guard Station, no date. Courtesy of North Carolina Travel and Tourism Department.

Cape Lookout Lighthouse and surrounding dunes, no date. Courtesy of Cape Lookout National Seashore.

Interior stairwell of Cape Lookout Lighthouse, 1977. Courtesy of Cape Lookout National Seashore.

View of Haig Point at sunset, 1994. Courtesy of Paul Barton.

Haig Point, Blodgett Room, 1997. Courtesy of Matthew Gardiner.

Harbour Town Lighthouse as seen from marina, 1996. Terrance Zepke.

Concrete base of former Cape Fear Lighthouse, 1996. Terrance Zepke.

sticks of dynamite were needed to demolish the massive, skeletal Cape Fear tower. All that's left to mark where it once stood are its concrete bases.

Before the lighthouse was blown up, the lens housing and prism reflectors from the lantern assembly were removed. Some reflectors currently sit atop a small lighthouse replica outside an antiques shop in Wilmington.

Old Baldy remained in service until 1935. The Fresnel lens was replaced with a radio beacon during World War II (1941). The beacon was useful to the U.S. Navy stationed across the river at Fort Caswell. The sentinel was sold to a private owner in 1963, who later sold it to the Carolina Cape Fear Corporation. The beacon was ultimately given to the Old Baldy Foundation, an organization dedicated to restoring the lighthouse and funded through private donations and state and federal grants.

To date, renovations to the lighthouse include replacing plaster on the exterior and putting a new copper roof on the lantern room. The wooden landing and stairs have also been repaired.

Fire destroyed the keeper's house in 1931 and the abandoned Coast Guard Station in 1968. However, the lighthouse survived and stands proudly near the marina entrance, greeting everyone who arrives on the island.

Photo of former Cape Fear Lighthouse generator shed, 1996. Built in 1903, it has a slate roof and 10-1/2" thick brick walls. Terrance Zepke.

On April 2, 1988, the Bald Head Island Lighthouse was relit by Geneva Smith, stepson of Captain Charles "Charlie" Swann, who manned the Cape Fear Lighthouse for about thirty years. Visitors can climb Old Baldy's 112 wooden steps to the top for a great view of the area.

A museum which would resemble the original keeper's cottage is planned to the east of the lighthouse. It will house artifacts and documents portraying Old Baldy's history. The Old Baldy Foundation hopes to start construction by the year 2000.

There are only two ways to reach the island: by the privately-owned passenger ferry or by private boat. Bald Head Island is accessible by a twenty-minute ferry ride from the terminal at Indigo Plantation Marina, in Southport, thirty miles south of Wilmington, NC, or sixty miles north of Myrtle Beach, SC. Ferry reservations should be made in advance and confirmed by calling 910-457-5003.

Visitors should plan to arrive at the ferry landing at least thirty minutes before departure time. Drive directly to the baggage area and unload luggage before parking car in the lot. A daily fee is charged for parking in secured lots. Payment is made upon exiting the lot.

Two of the three former Cape Fear Lighthouse keeper's cottages (Cap'n Charlie's) before renovations, 1971. Courtesy of North Carolina State Archives.

For more information on how to get to Bald Head Island by private boat, call the dockmaster at 910-457-7380 or the transportation office at 910-457-5006, or listen to VHF channel 16.

Directions: To reach Southport, take 211 South, turn right onto West 9th Street, and follow the road about one and a half miles to Indigo Plantation. The road dead-ends into the ferry terminal, where there are indoor and covered outdoor waiting areas, restrooms, and a ticket office.

NOTE: Once on the island, transportation is by tram, golf cart, bicycle, or foot. Accommodations are available at a bed-and-breakfast, an inn, several condominiums, and rental houses. Each furnishes golf carts and/or bicycles for use on the island.

NOTE: There are two ferry terminals in Southport: one is the state ferry to Fort Fisher on East Moore Street, and the other is Bald Head Island Ferry Landing at Indigo Plantation Marina.

Other Points of Interest

The former **Lifesaving Station boathouse** (Bald Head Creek), used by boats bringing in supplies to the Lifesaving Station and Cape Fear Lighthouse, is now a private residence.

Three cottages, known as **Cap'n Charlie's Station** (1903), are now used as rental accommodations. The cottages originally housed Captain Charles Swann, as well as his assistants and their families. The cottages are listed in the National Register of Historic Places.

Useful Addresses and Resources

Bald Head Island Information Center
5079 Southport-Supply Road
Southport, NC 28461
1-800-432-RENT

Old Baldy Foundation (Bald Head Island Lighthouse)
P.O. Box 3007
Bald Head Island, NC 28461
910-799-4640

Southport Chamber of Commerce
4841 Long Beach Road SE
Southport, NC 28461
910-457-6964

Southport Maritime Museum
116 N. Howe St.
P.O. Box 11101
Southport, NC 28461
910-457-0003

FRYING PAN LIGHT TOWER

Fast Facts

- Frying Pan Light Tower is named for a body of water in eastern Tyrrell County roughly shaped like a frying pan.
- The station is fitted with oceanographic equipment.
- The tower is sometimes referred to as a "Texas" tower since it resembles the steel structures found in offshore Texas oil drilling.

The Frying Pan Light Tower was built to accompany the Oak Island Lighthouse, a modern beacon lit in 1958. The tower was needed to warn Wilmington-bound ships of Cape Fear's many sandbars and channels.

Before the light tower (or lightstation), there were several lightships that served the dangerous Frying Pan Shoals area. The first was put into place in 1854, but was removed during the Civil War. From 1865 until 1966, many lightships bearing the name "Frying Pan" were stationed near Cape Fear. Each was eventually removed: some suffered storm damage; others needed repairs when they broke loose from their moorings or were rammed by passing ships. The last lightship was removed from service because of concerns that a hurricane would eventually shake it from its moorings.

Construction on the current massive, $2 million tower began in 1964, and in 1966, it officially replaced the Frying Pan Shoals Lightship. The "house" was transported by barge from Louisiana to the Frying Pan Shoals area, thirty-two and a half miles southeast of Cape Fear. It was lifted and attached to the foundation by a huge crane.

The structure is supported by four steel posts, each measuring

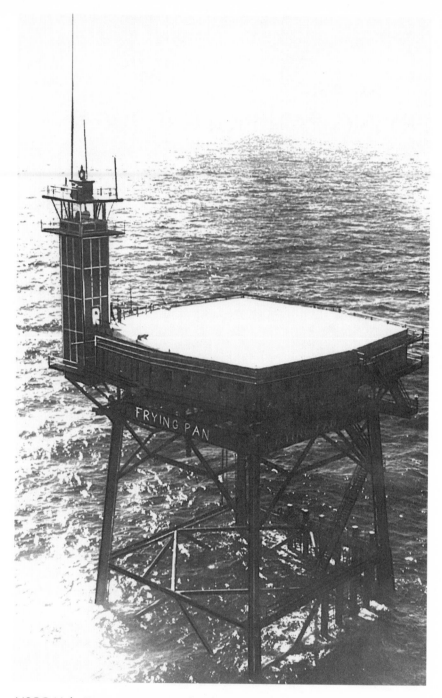

USCG Light Tower Frying Pan Shoals, ca. 1980. Courtesy of North Carolina State Archives.

90   Lighthouses of North Carolina

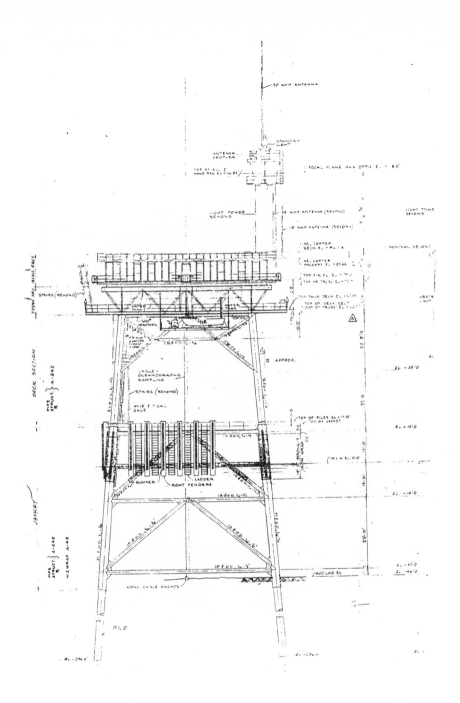

Photocopy of print of Frying Pan Lightstation, no date. Courtesy of United States Coast Guard, Fort Macon.

Frying Pan Light Tower   91

Photocopy of Frying Pan Lightship as seen on April 30, 1972. The ship served from 1854 to 1864. Courtesy of North Carolina State Archives.

forty-two inches in diameter. Its steel legs extend almost 296 feet below sea level to securely anchor the 555-ton house.

On the lower levels are the boat and tank decks, where fuel and a lifeboat are stored. Seventy-five feet above water is the Quarters Deck, a 8,100-square-foot deck that comprised the crew's living area and work and machinery spaces. Above this is the Helo Deck, a helicopter pad which doubled as an exercise and recreation area. Eighty-six feet above water, the Helo Deck is also where the station's fresh water was collected in 22,000 gallon cisterns.

The lighthouse itself juts out of the top deck's southeast corner, extending another 33 feet and presenting a focal plane of 118 feet above sea level.

Like Diamond Shoals Light Tower, this structure was manned by six Coast Guard personnel. The rotation called for four crew members to stay onboard while two had shore leave. Duty was two weeks on and one week off. The Officer-in-Charge was a Boatswain's Mate, First Class. Other crew members were two Machinery Technicians, Second Class; one Electronics Technician, Third Class; one Electrician's Mate, Third Class; and one Fireman. As of November 1979, the "Texas" tower became permanently automated, and personnel are no longer necessary.

The original lighting apparatus was a DCB-224 optic, which gave off 448,800 candlepower, and had a range of up to twenty miles. The current lighting system, which runs on solar power, was activated on February 20, 1996. It consists of eight thirty-five-watt solar panels that charge a twelve-volt lead-acid storage battery. This system powers a VEGA VRB-25 rotating beacon with a fifty-watt, twelve-volt lamp, equaling 58,000 candlepower. The flash pattern is one white flash every six seconds. A Fresnel lens adds visibility by extending the light's range to over sixteen miles on a clear night. A back-up system includes a forty-five-watt solar panel, a twelve-volt nickel-cadmium battery, and two 250mm lanterns. Additionally, a twelve-volt foghorn can be heard one mile away.

Although mainly a navigational aid, the station is also fitted with oceanographic equipment that measures wave height and frequency, and water temperature, speed, and direction. Wind and air speed and direction can also be determined.

As with Diamond Shoals Light Tower, the Frying Pan Light Tower took a beating a few years ago from Hurricane Fran. Forty-seven foot waves did so much damage to the boat level that it is no longer safe to use. The light station can be reached only by helicopter.

Major Coast Guard inspections take place twice a year. The US Coast Guard Aids-to-Navigation Team in Fort Macon also performs quarterly maintenance. Routine helicopter operations allow for frequent visual inspections, and the structure is always checked after big storms.

The future looks grim for this light station. While it is presently listed in "fair to good condition," it will cease operations in 2004, when the Coast Guard plans to decommission all D5 towers. However, the Coast Guard is exploring various options, such as private leasing of the tower, once the station is discontinued.

Directions: The Frying Pan Light Tower is located in the open ocean and is not open to the public.

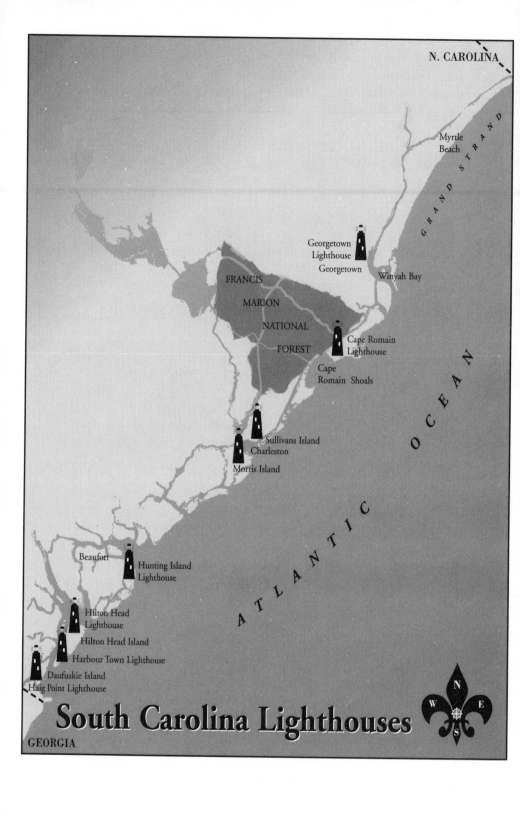

South Carolina Lighthouses

LIGHTHOUSES
OF
SOUTH CAROLINA

*Anythin' for a quiet life, as the man said
wen he took the sitivation at the lighthouse.*

— Charles Dickens (1812-1870),
excerpted from *The Pickwick Papers*

1767 — Old Charleston, Morris Island
1801 — Georgetown
1812 — Georgetown rebuilt
1827 — Cape Romain
1858 — New Cape Romain
1859 — Hunting Island
1863 — Hilton Head
1867 — Georgetown rebuilt
1869 — Hilton Head rebuilt
1873 — Haig Point
1873 — Daufuskie Island
1875 — Hunting Island rebuilt
1876 — Old Charleston rebuilt
1887 — Hunting Island dismantled
1889 — Hunting Island relocated and relit
1962 — New Charleston, Sullivan's Island
1970 — Harbour Town

GEORGETOWN LIGHTHOUSE

Fast Facts

- Eighty-seven feet tall, Georgetown is South Carolina's oldest active lighthouse.
- Since 1986, the light has remained on both day and night.
- Georgetown is named for George I, King of England.

Georgetown, established in 1732, is the third oldest port in South Carolina. At one time it exported more rice than any other port in the world. As commerce increased, a lighthouse was needed to guide vessels into the harbor or to help get them safely past the peninsula between the Waccamaw River and the Atlantic Ocean.

In 1789, a local businessman named Paul Trapier donated a tract of land for the tower. But because the federal government assumed responsibility for all navigational aids the following year, it was several years before the area got its much-needed lighthouse. The delay was due to several factors, but at the heart of the matter was good old-fashioned politics. Although the lighthouses scattered along the coast of the Carolinas were critical for navigation, the government gave first consideration to the needs and desires of the more affluent northern communities.

Finally, on February 28, 1795, the government bought a parcel of land and released $5000 to build the tower. Construction didn't begin until 1799, and it wasn't until two years later that the Georgetown Lighthouse was lit.

The lighthouse was erected on North Island, which is at the entrance to Winyah Bay and Georgetown. For this reason, the simple seventy-two foot wooden structure was sometimes referred to as the North Island Lighthouse. The tower base was twenty-six feet across,

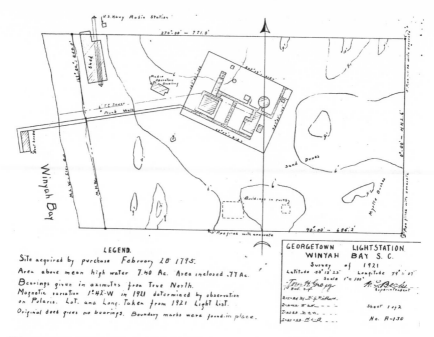

Diagram of lighthouse site, 1921 survey. Courtesy of National Archives.

and the lantern was approximately six feet in diameter. Since quite a few North and South Carolinians used to make their living providing whale products, it's not surprising that the beacon was fueled by cheap and plentiful whale oil. Only five short years after it was first illuminated, the tower was demolished by a storm.

The structure was rebuilt in 1812. Also seventy-two feet high, the new tower was made of brick and painted white. During the Civil War, Confederates used the beacon as an observation post until it was captured by Union soldiers in May 1862.

Having sustained severe damage during the Civil War, the harbor light was rebuilt for the last time in 1867. The whitewashed brick structure now stands eighty-seven feet tall, with a focal plane of eighty-five feet. The tower base is twenty feet in diameter, with six-inch-thick walls. The beacon has stone support posts, and its 124 stone steps lead to a watch area and lantern room, which once housed a 4th-order Fresnel lens.

A white picket fence enclosed the lighthouse, along with several outbuildings including an oil house, cistern, and two-story wood-frame keeper's quarters. The area also has an old U.S. Navy radio station and dormitory that was used by the Navy radio operators.

Georgetown Lighthouse as it looks today. Courtesy of Georgetown County Chamber of Commerce.

Keeper's house, oil shed, and lighthouse as they looked on April 22, 1893. Courtesy of National Archives.

Georgetown was manned by the U.S. Coast Guard until 1986, when the light was automated. Today it is equipped with a 3500-candlepower light magnified through a 5th-order Fresnel lens, visible over twelve miles away. The light runs day and night because it lacks a timing mechanism, but the U.S. Coast Guard decided this was more economical than the high cost of installing such a mechanism. There are also two back-up lights powered by battery packs.

Directions: The tower is located on North Island, a fifteen-mile-long wildlife refuge. Land has been cleared around the lighthouse, but the rest of the refuge remains untouched. The island, a short boat ride from Georgetown, can be reached from Georgetown's Shrine launching ramp on Boulevard Street. South Island, also a wildlife refuge, allows a good view of the lighthouse. Call the Yawkey Wildlife Center at 843-546-6814 to schedule a tour (Tuesdays 3-6 P.M.) via private ferry to South Island. Tours, which can accommodate up to 14 people, must be booked 3–6 months in advance.

GEORGETOWN LIGHTHOUSE KEEPER'S DAUGHTER: A Ghost Story

No one lived on North Island but the keeper and his daughter. The man had to row to Georgetown for provisions, and often took the young girl. One day on their return home, a rainstorm began and the sea became treacherous. The keeper continued rowing, trying to keep his small boat afloat, when a wave knocked the little girl out of the boat.

Although the keeper tried desperately to find his daughter among the waves, she disappeared and drowned. The distraught father was rescued but was never the same. He never again left North Island: local fisherman brought him supplies and checked on him until his death. Shortly afterwards, boaters began seeing a man and a little girl rowing around the island, but whenever anyone got close to their dinghy, it disappeared! Locals came to understand that a sighting of these ghosts signaled the approach of a severe storm, and they heeded its warning.

Other Points of Interest

Full and half-day tours. Georgetown's large historic district, as well as Shell Island, Black River Rice Plantation, and much more, can be seen during tours given virtually year-round. Also, the area has numerous outdoor activities and year-round festivals.

The Rice Museum. Housed in the Old Market Building and part of the Historic District, the museum is also known as the "Big Ben" of Georgetown because of the huge clock mounted on the front of the building. The museum has displays relating to the old rice plantation days.

633 Front Street on Harborwalk
Georgetown, SC 29442
843-546-7432

The Kaminski House Museum. Built in 1769, the museum is recognized as a pre-Revolutionary War landmark. Originally owned by Paul Trapier II, a wealthy businessman known as the "King of Georgetown", it houses antiques such as a fifteenth century Spanish wedding chest.

1003 Front Street
Georgetown, SC 29442
843-546-7706

The Georgetown Tour Company. The tour company offers a Historic City Tour, along with a Ghostbusting Tour and Afternoon Tea 'n Tour (by reservation only; group must be at least twelve to fifteen people).

627 Front Street
Georgetown, SC 29442
843-546-6827

Capt. Sandy's Tours. Capt. Sandy's offers Georgetown Lighthouse tours, Plantation Excursions (former rice planters' mansions), Shell Island Tour (a barrier island with great shell-collecting, and Natural History (swamps and backwater channels).

Broad and Front Street on Harborwalk
Georgetown, SC 29442
843-527-4106

Swamp Fox Tours II. Swamp Fox offers tours of the National Register's Historic District.

1001 Front Street
Georgetown, SC 29442
843-527-6469

The Jolly Rover Sailing Schooner. The crew appears in pirate garb and tells pirate stories and other local lore, while the boat takes a day or sunset cruise along Winyah Bay.

Broad and Front Street at Harborwalk
Georgetown, SC 29442
800-705-9063/843-546-8822

Useful Addresses and Resources

Georgetown Chamber of Commerce
P.O. Box 1776
Georgetown, SC 29442
843-546-8436
800-777-7705

Georgetown Charters
109 W. Alder Street
Andrews, SC 29510
843-545-5479
Offers expeditions to lighthouse and surrounding areas.

CAPE ROMAIN LIGHTHOUSES

Fast Facts

- The two towers are a rare exception to the "twin tower" rule, meaning the original was not destroyed when the second was built.
- The lighthouses are part of the 65,000-acre Cape Romain National Wildlife Refuge, established in 1932.
- Cape Romain was most likely named by the Spanish in honor of St. Romano, on whose birthday the cape was discovered.

On March 3, 1823, the United States Treasury released funds for a tower on Lighthouse Island, formerly known as Raccoon Key. A stone building that was once a windmill was to be bought and adapted to serve as a lighthouse. But a thorough investigation showed that the area overflowed at high tide, so erosion would plague the structure.

Another more suitable site was found on the island, but this parcel of land was supposedly owned by twelve people. Between a title dispute and the negotiations over compensation for the Northeast Key of Raccoon Key, there was a lengthy delay in construction. Finally, the tower was completed in 1827. Its total cost of $8,425 included its lighting system and keeper's quarters.

A timber piling foundation supports the simple round brick tower. The structure is unadorned, from its wooden steps to the window trim and framing. The tower's base has a diameter of almost thirty feet at its bottom, which decreases to fifteen feet at the top. The tower was painted black and white.

At eighty-seven feet above sea level, the light was supposed to be visible up to eighteen miles away. But mariners complained the

Old Cape Romain Tower, 1913. Courtesy of National Archives.

MURDER AT CAPE ROMAIN

One of the keepers at Cape Romain Lighthouse was a Norwegian named Fischer. He loved the desolate isle and his duties as keeper, but, unfortunately, his wife did not share his enthusiasm for their new lifestyle. She was miserable and homesick for her native Norway, her family, and her friends. She begged her husband to let her make an extended visit to Norway, but he refused. The couple quarreled frequently about the issue until she told him she was going. Fischer was so enraged that his wife would not accept the word of her husband as "law" that he stabbed her to death with a kitchen knife.

Fischer told the few people he spoke to that his wife had committed suicide. No one suspected the truth until the keeper confessed his terrible secret on his deathbed. Subsequent keepers tended the woman's grave after that, pulling up weeds and planting flowers. It is said that drops of blood mysteriously appeared on the keeper's cottage floorboards—at the exact site of the woman's murder—until the lighthouse was decommissioned and the dwelling no longer existed.

beacon wasn't bright enough, so in 1847 it was refitted with a fixed light of eleven lamps and reflectors. However, the squat tower built near the entrance of the Santee River never fulfilled its duty of helping vessels avoid the hazardous nine-mile Cape Romain shoals and southern Gulf Stream.

The Lighthouse Board approved a taller, more modern lighthouse to be built at the same site. The lighting apparatus was removed from the original beacon and it was decommissioned in 1858. Remarkably, even after the second lighthouse went into service, the first tower wasn't destroyed. Older structures were generally removed so they wouldn't confuse seamen or become hazards if storms or erosion swept pieces of the tower out to sea. The two towers somehow became an exception to this rule.

It was discovered during construction of the second beacon that its walls were out of plumb. Its concrete foundation had settled on one side, putting the tower almost twenty-four inches from the vertical. This structural shortcoming was never corrected, so the 150-foot octagonal tower leans slightly. This second tower was later

Cape Romain keeper's quarters, 1827–1858. Courtesy of National Archives.

painted white with alternating black and white vertical stripes covering the upper two thirds.

The lantern room contained a 1st-order Fresnel lens, positioned at a focal plane of 161 feet, which allowed a visibility of roughly nineteen miles out to sea. Both the lens and lantern room were damaged during the Civil War, but were repaired in 1866. The lighting was replaced again in 1931, this time with a revolving bull's-eye lens blanketing a 500-watt bulb, which was illuminated by the island's new generating plant. In 1937, that apparatus was replaced with an automated thousand-candlepower beam.

The older tower was painted red in 1937 (so it wouldn't be confused with the working lighthouse) and used as a storage facility. All of the windows and lighting apparatus have been vandalized or removed, so nothing of the original equipment remains. The wooden stairwell was also removed, and only the bottom third of the structure still exists. The Coast Guard replaced the newer lighthouse with lighted buoys in 1947. Records indicate that all of the outbuildings were destroyed that same year, with one exception. The keeper's

Cape Romain towers and keeper's house, 1893. Courtesy of National Archives.

house was left intact, but removed in the late 1950s. Even the generating plant is no longer on the island.

A 195-step iron spiral stairway leads to the lantern room of the newer structure, which still has its revolving platform, exterior balcony with railing, and circular brass roof. Despite the fact that the tower has settled over the years, which has created several cracks in the structure, the lighthouse is still in good shape. Although the area was hit hard several years ago by Hurricane Hugo, the second tower still seems to be holding its own. With the help of volunteers, the Cape Romain Wildlife Refuge has recently repainted the exterior and is weatherproofing the doors and windows.

Located on seventy-five-acre Lighthouse Island, the towers are currently owned by the U.S. Fish and Wildlife Service. Boaters along this part of the Intracoastal Waterway use them as a visual mark in daylight.

Directions: The Cape Romain Lighthouses are located on Lighthouse Island, approximately forty minutes by boat from the nearest

Both Cape Romain Towers, 1997. Terrance Zepke.

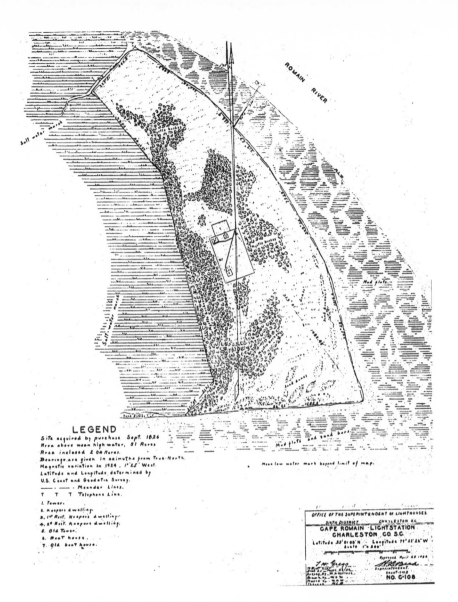

Diagram of Lighthouse Island and layout of lighthouse compound, 1924. Courtesy of National Archives.

town, McClellanville. McClellanville is approximately thirty-five miles north of Charleston (US 17), and thirty-three miles south of Georgetown (US 17). There is a boat launch for private boats located at the town hall. However, the towers are closed to the public and cannot be reached except by wading through water and heavy mud. (There is no dock and a boat cannot get too close to the island due to the shoals.) Boaters should know that markers are scarce, and it is easy to get lost on this inner waterway. One company, Coastal Expeditions, charters small boats to Lighthouse Island.

NOTE: Once on the island, there is nothing to see but the towers and there are no restrooms. Low tides create a small window of time during the day when the island can be approached for exploring. Be aware that the island is not accommodating to visitors: its vegetation has not been tended in many years, and insects are more than plentiful.

Other Points of Interest

Bull Island. Reached by a twenty-minute ferry ride, Bull Island is part of the 65,000-acre Cape Romain Wildlife Refuge. It hosts 250 species of birds, as well as red wolves, alligators, and other wildlife. En route, see schools of dolphin and more of the magnificent refuge. Coastal Expeditions runs a pontoon boat to Bull Island (three miles offshore) in the morning and again in the afternoon.

McClellanville. Ask anyone who's been there and he'll tell you McClellanville is "the prettiest town you'll ever see". I agree. I stopped there after visiting the lighthouses, and caught the end of their Annual Shrimp Festival. I also drove around admiring some of the beautiful waterfront homes.

Georgetown and Charleston. These historic towns are close to the Cape Romain lighthouses.

Useful Addresses and Resources

Cape Romain Refuge Manager
5821 Highway 17 N (twenty miles north of Charleston)
Awendaw, SC 29429
843-928-3368

Charleston Area Convention & Visitors Bureau
P.O. Box 975
Charleston, SC 29402
843-853-8000
800-868-8118

Coastal Expeditions, Inc. (private ferry service)
514-B Mill St.
Mt. Pleasant, SC 29464
843-881-4582

NOTE: Ferry service operates under exclusive contract with the U.S. Fish & Wildlife Service. This means no other company can take passengers into this area of Cape Romain Wildlife Refuge. Ask for Captain Randy.

Francis Marion National Forest
(site of joint visitor center for Francis Marion National Forest and Cape Romain Wildlife Refuge, with camping available)
U.S. Highway 17 (eighteen miles from Charleston)
843-928-3368

Georgetown Chamber of Commerce
and
Georgetown County Convention and Visitors Bureau
P.O. Box 1776
Georgetown, SC 29442
843-546-8436/800-777-7705

MORRIS ISLAND LIGHTHOUSE

Fast Facts

- The original Charleston Lighthouse was built by order of King George III of England.
- The present lighthouse was built in 1876.
- The lighthouse has endured just about every form of damage Mother Nature could throw at it, including earthquakes, hurricanes, and erosion.

Historically called the Charleston Main Light but now more commonly known as Morris Island Lighthouse, this 161-foot conical brick tower beacon stands six miles southeast of Charleston, South Carolina's biggest port.

At the time of the Revolution, Morris Island was a four-mile stretch of land separating Folly Island and Sullivan's Island. Morris Island was actually three distinct islands called Middle Bay, Morrison, and Cummings Point. (Middle Bay was near Folly Island, Morrison was in the middle, and Cummings Point overlooked the Charleston Harbor entrance.) Records reveal that in 1673 baskets laden with "fier" balls and oakum illuminated the shore. Tallow candles replaced this method in 1716. In 1767, King George III of England ordered a tower to be placed at this site.

The first Charleston lighthouse was built on Middle Bay, now Morris Island. It was one of only two lighthouses south of the Delaware Bay to survive the Revolutionary War (the other was at Tybee Island, Georgia). Designed by Samuel Cardy and built by Adam Miller, aided by engineer Thomas Young, the finished product was a 102-foot, tubular brick tower whose light was fueled by lard oil. At 125 feet above sea level, the revolving lamp had a range of twelve miles. A plaque

1876 Government survey done under direction of W.A. Jones, Captain of Engineers. Courtesy of National Archives.

(which no longer exists) was attached to the lighthouse that read, "The first stone of this beacon was laid on the 30 of May 1767 in the seventh year of his Majesty's Reign, George the III."

When the federal government took control of all navigational aids in 1790, Middle Bay, the lighthouse, a one-room keeper's house, and

Morris Island Lighthouse showing keeper's house and equipment shed, as well as a retaining wall, ca. 1900. Courtesy of National Archives.

all outbuildings became government property. Soon after that, the channel shifted and incoming tide waters blocked the inlets that separated the three little islands. This created one big island called Morrison (later shortened to Morris) Island.

In 1858, a 1st-order Fresnel lens was installed. Three years later, on a chilly January morning, the first shot of the Civil War was fired from Morris Island. Later that year, fleeing Confederate soldiers blew up the lighthouse so Union soldiers couldn't use it.

An 1876 government survey, made under the direction of W.A. Jones, Captain of Engineers for the Sixth District, is at the National Archives. It shows there were also two pairs of range lights and keeper's houses on Morris Island. One faced the Atlantic; the other, Lighthouse Inlet.

Although an exhaustive search of state and national archives, the U.S. Coast Guard Historian's Office, the *1994 Inventory of Historic Light Stations,* the South Carolina State Library, the Charleston Historical Society, the Charleston Museum, and the National Maritime Initiative concluded that there were no other lights besides the main beacon, two archived images dated circa 1885 seem to indicate the presence of range lights on Morris Island. When these other lights were built, and what happened to them, remains a mystery. One guess is that the beacons were wiped out during the big 1885 hurricane, and

Morris Island Range Light, ca. 1885 Courtesy of National Archives.

were not rebuilt because the channels had shifted and the lights were no longer needed. The *1994 Inventory of Historic Light Stations* does list other lights in the area, but either their descriptions or their dates do not match what little information I have uncovered about these beacons.

In 1873, Congress made appropriations to rebuild the lighthouse destroyed during the Civil War. Three years later, the Charleston Main Light, costing almost $150,000, was erected. Because of the shifting channel, it was placed about 400 yards southeast of the earlier tower. Built on pilings secured fifty feet below ground, it has an eight-foot-thick foundation with a diameter of thirty-three feet at the base, decreasing to sixteen feet eight inches at the top. Acetylene was used to light the 1st-order Fresnel lens, which was visible to ships up to nineteen miles away.

The 161-foot conical tower was designed to mimic North Carolina's Bodie Island and Currituck Lighthouses, and it was even painted with black and white horizontal striping, the same pattern as Bodie Island Lighthouse. At alternate levels on the east and west of the lighthouse are arched windows. Iron steps spiral up nine stories to the lantern room, which has an external gallery and iron parapet.

Three caretakers—the keeper and his two assistants—lived in the three-story keepers' dwelling with their families. These families made up a small community. There were fifteen buildings at this site in the late 1800s, including keepers' residence, numerous outbuildings, and even a one-room schoolhouse. A teacher for the

Morris Island Range Light, no date. Courtesy of National Archives.

children was brought over by rowboat on Mondays and returned to the mainland on Fridays. The community kept livestock and also maintained a vegetable garden.

Natural disasters, including an 1885 hurricane and an 1886 earthquake, created big cracks in the lighthouse. The impact of World War II bombing practice on nearby Folly Island worsened these cracks.

The shifting channel required that jetties be built to save Charleston Harbor. The jetties were completed in 1889, and caused erosion damage to Morris Island. The subsequent structural cracks and loss of land caused the lighthouse to lean somewhat, and this reduced the light's range. By the end of 1938, the Coast Guard had relocated the keepers, moved some of the buildings, and destroyed the rest so that tides couldn't eventually carry debris to the Atlantic Ocean and create a hazard to mariners. That same year, the lighthouse was automated and the 1st-order Fresnel lens removed. The lens was subsequently sold at auction.

Morris Island Lighthouse 117

"Ruins of Old Charleton Lighthouse on Morris Island." Temporary light installed by occupying Federal troops during summer of 1863 during War Between the States. Courtesy of To Take Charleston: The Civil War on Folly Island *by James W. Hagy. Charleston, WV: Pictorial Histories Publishing Company, 1993.*

Since that time, over 1600 feet of land around the tower has been lost to erosion. When the Sullivan's Island Lighthouse was built in 1962, the Morris Island structure was no longer used and was destined to be destroyed. The Coast Guard, fearing that the lighthouse would fall into the water at some point and become a navigational danger, wanted to tear it down. However, local residents (including a former keeper's relative) formed a nonprofit group called the Charleston Preservation Society to prevent this from happening. The organization petitioned Congress to keep the Morris Island Lighthouse intact, and their efforts paid off. The Coast Guard put an underground steel wall around the tower to protect it from further erosion damage.

Today, the abandoned beacon serves as a daytime visual marker. It has become its own island in the Atlantic, with bits of its foundation periodically flaking off and sliding into the water. The stairs are rusted but mostly intact. Window panes are missing from storm damage, and vandals have removed the skylights. However, the iron- and stone-work in the lantern gallery and around windows can still be seen. Overall, the tower is considered to be in good shape.

The structure is privately owned by S.E. Felkil of Yelsen Land

*Original Charleston
Lighthouse, ca. 1767.
Courtesy of* To Take
Charleston: The Civil War
on Folly Island *by James W.
Hagy. Charleston, WV:
Pictorial Histories Publishing
Company, 1993.*

Company, Incorporated. Visitors can get a good view of the lighthouse from Folly Beach on James Island, or can travel close to Morris Island by private boat (there are numerous boat launches at Charleston and Mt. Pleasant). However, the "island" consists only of the lighthouse and its crumbling foudation, and there's no room for visitors to dock a boat or walk.

Directions: There are no signs indicating Morris Island or the lighthouse. Take SC 171 to James Island and Folly Beach. Turn left onto East Ashley Street at the last red light before the oceanfront Holiday Inn, and follow this road until it dead-ends. There is a parking area on the right three houses back from the beach. Proceed on foot for about a half mile. The lighthouse can be seen about 300 yards offshore.

NOTE: Beware of mosquitoes and sand fleas!

Other Points of Interest

The Charleston Museum. This, the "oldest established museum collection in North America," has incredible exhibits detailing Charleston's history. The displays include photographs, vehicles, furniture, silver, and even a replica of *H. L. Hunley*, a submarine used during a Civil War blockade of Charleston Harbor.

Charleston Museum
360 Meeting Street
Charleston, SC 29405
843-722-2996

Sightseeing tours. Tours of the city's historic district, Boone Hall Plantation (used by many television and film crews), the Battery, Charles Pinckney Historic Site, and other historic sites can be taken by horse-drawn carriage, foot, bus, or automobile.

Cruise around scenic Charleston Harbor. See Fort Sumter, a man-made island. There are also tours of the fort, where visitors can hear about what it was like to serve there.

Visit Charleston's other fort, Fort Moultrie, and Patriots Point Naval Museum.
Patriots Point is known as the world's largest naval and maritime collection, which includes the World War II aircraft carrier USS *Yorktown;* the destroyer, USS *Laffey;* as well as submarines, Coast Guard cutters, and much more.

Useful Addresses and Resources

"Car" Go Tour Lines
843-449-7366

Charleston Area Convention & Visitors Bureau
P. O. Box 975
Charleston, SC 29402
843-853-8000 or 800-868-8118
The Visitors Bureau will send the *Charleston Area Visitors Guide* and information packet to prospective visitors.

SULLIVAN'S ISLAND LIGHTHOUSE

Fast Facts

- Sullivan's Island Lighthouse, erected in 1962, was the last tower built in the state.
- This sentinel replaced the old Morris Island Lighthouse.
- It has the potential to be one of the most powerful lights in the world.

Information is scarce on some of the early range lights and simple light structures, but the National Maritime Initiative's archeological database and the U.S. Coast Guard Historian's Office records show a small light tower marking Charleston's channel entrance before the Sullivan's Island Lighthouse. The red square structure was erected in 1848, and stood on four brick piers. It was positioned three hundred yards southwest of Fort Moultrie. The fixed white light was a 6th-order Fresnel lens with a range of ten and a quarter miles. It was rebuilt in 1872.

Another beacon was added in 1888 to make the pair of range lights known as Sullivan's Island Range Lights. The newer tower served as the rear light, and was approximately 690 feet from the Sullivan's Island Front Light. The rear light was a fixed red reflector light, positioned thirty-three feet above water. Its base was a black skeletal structure, square at the base and rising in a pyramid-shaped tower. On May 20, 1899, the lights were renamed South Channel Range Lights.

In 1962, shifting of the channel marking Charleston Harbor necessitated the building of one of the last lighthouses in America ever to be constructed. The new Charleston lighthouse was built on the north side of the harbor. Originally, the tower was painted orange and white, but was later changed to black and white.

Sullivan's Island Lighthouse, 1996. Terrance Zepke.

Anchored by steel girders and a concrete foundation, the modern tower is in stark contrast to older lighthouses. This 163-foot beacon, built for extra protection from hurricanes, has an unusual shape and triangular aluminum paneling. It also has many modern advantages, such as an elevator which goes most of the way up. (It is the only lighthouse in the United States with an elevator.) It also has stairs, which must be used to enter the lantern room. Because it contains offices, the interior is air conditioned. A generator is located in the tower's base.

Tower of former keeper's house. Restored and currently used by Coast Guard personnel, 1996. Terrance Zepke.

When it was first illuminated on June 15, 1962, the lighting system was very different from that which is currently being used. With its 28,000,000-candlepower capability, Sullivan's Island was probably one of the most powerful lights in the world. However, the six-lamp lighting apparatus was not only more than was needed, but was also hazardous, so it was modified in 1967. Three low-intensity lamps are now used, reducing the candlepower to 1,170,000. These

Sullivan's Island Range Light (possibly front light), no date. Courtesy of National Archives.

lights have a range of twenty-six miles and are rotated by an automated system that was put in place in 1982. A back-up system was also installed at the same time. The lights shine day and night. One bulb blinks every five seconds, the second every twenty seconds, and the third every thirty seconds.

Sullivan's Island Lighthouse is part of a Coast Guard compound and is therefore not open to the public. The South Carolina Parks Department, supervisors of nearby Fort Moultrie, share the lighthouse's offices with the Coast Guard. Also within the compound is an old boathouse, keeper's house and storage building from the former Lifesaving Station (South Carolina's only rescue station). The structures have been restored and are currently being used by Coast Guard personnel. They are listed on the National Register of Historic Places.

Directions: Take US 17 or I-526 to SC 703 through Mt. Pleasant to Sullivan's Island. The lighthouse is easily seen near Fort Moultrie, on the left behind a locked gate.

Sullivan's Island Range Light (possibly rear light), no date. Courtesy of National Archives.

NOTE: Sullivan's Island is reached by drawbridge so during summer months there could be traffic delays.

Other Points of Interest

The Charleston Museum. This, the "oldest established museum collection in North America," has incredible exhibits detailing Charleston's history. The displays include photographs, vehicles, furniture, silver, and even a replica of *H. L. Hunley*, a submarine used during a Civil War blockade of Charleston Harbor.

Charleston Museum
360 Meeting Street
Charleston, SC 29405
843-722-2996

Sightseeing tours. Tours of the city's historic district, Boone Hall Plantation (used by many television and film crews), the Battery, Charles Pinckney Historic Site, and other historic sites can be taken by horse-drawn carriage, foot, bus, or automobile.

Cruise around scenic Charleston Harbor. See Fort Sumter, a man-made island. There are also tours of the fort, where visitors can hear about what it was like to serve at the fort.

Visit Charleston's other fort, Fort Moultrie, and Patriots Point Naval Museum.
Patriots Point is known as the world's largest naval and maritime collection, which includes the World War II aircraft carrier USS *Yorktown;* the destroyer, USS *Laffey;* as well as submarines, Coast Guard cutters, and much more.

Useful Addresses and Resources

"Car" Go Tour Lines
843-449-7366

Charleston Area Convention & Visitors Bureau
P. O. Box 975
Charleston, SC 29402
843-853-8000 or 800-868-8118
The Visitors Bureau will send the *Charleston Area Visitors Guide* and information packet to prospective visitors.

HUNTING ISLAND LIGHTHOUSE

Fast Facts

- The first Hunting Island Lighthouse was built in 1859; the current lighthouse is a cast-iron tower erected in 1875.
- The beacon is located in the 5,000-acre Hunting Island State Park.
- Hunting Island is part of a chain of islands considered "a sportsman's idea of Paradise."

This seacoast light was very important for guiding vessels from South Carolina's major harbors of Charleston and Beaufort to Georgia's main port of Savannah. Just one look at an interior geological survey shows the heavy concentration of sand and mud all along the coastline around this area.

According to a March 8, 1859 "Notice to Mariners" by W.H.C. Whiting, Captain of the Corps of Engineers (U.S.A.), a Hunting Island Light Station was to be built and lit by year's end. By order of the Lighthouse Board, the main lighthouse would be a ninety-five-foot "conical tower built of reddish gray brick, surmounted by a brass lantern." The lantern would house a revolving 2nd-order Fresnel lens with a focal plane of 108 feet above the sea. The light would flash every thirty seconds, and its range would be seventeen miles. The smaller beacon light would be an "open-work wooden frame, painted white, 32 feet high." Its focal plane would be thirty-nine feet above the sea, and the fixed light would encase a 6th-order Fresnel lens. According to Mike Walker of the South Carolina State Park Service, however, this second structure may not have actually been built.

The Hunting Island Light Station was officially put into service

Former keeper's house foundation (uncovered in 1995), as seen from top of tower, 1996. Terrance Zepke.

on July 1, 1859 at the north end of Hunting Island, but within a few years it no longer existed. It was destroyed during the Civil War.

A replacement structure made of cast iron plates—each weighing 1,200 pounds—was built further inland, about a quarter mile from the shore. Construction was delayed by crew illness, most likely malaria, but the $102,000 project was finally completed in 1875. Its brilliant white light came from a 100,000-candlepower beam that flashed every thirty seconds. The lamp was lit by kerosene and was reflected through a 2nd-order Fresnel lens. The light had a focal distance of 132.6 feet above sea level. (Often, publications give conflicting measurements for the height of a light-

Lantern room prisms, 1996. Terrance Zepke.

house. This doesn't necessarily mean a source is incorrect, but more likely that in each source the height was measured from a different point. For instance, Hunting Island Lighthouse is 108 feet if measured from the observation deck, but 127 feet if measured from the lantern room.)

A keeper and two assistants were needed to man this sentinel, so an impressive three-story house was built. The sixty-three by thirty-eight foot dwelling had twelve rooms, so it could comfortably shelter all of the keepers' families. An oil shed and two storage buildings were also erected nearby.

The structural ingenuity of this tower was that it was moveable in case erosion became too great a problem. It did (roughly 440 feet of erosion occurred during just one season), and jetties and revetments were built to slow the erosion process. However, in 1889, less than fifteen years after it was first lit, the lighthouse had to be disassembled and transported about a mile and a quarter south of its original location.

Perched on its new foundation, the tower was relit on October 1, 1889. If you look closely at the brick interior, you can still see the numbers used to help builders reassemble the tower. The total cost of the relocation was only $51,000, much less than what it would have cost to build a new lighthouse. Later that year, the other struc-

Close-up of upper portion of Hunting Island beacon, 1996. Terrance Zepke.

Hunting Island tower, 1996. Terrance Zepke.

Storage building, 1996. Terrance Zepke.

tures were also moved, and a boathouse, tram, and dock were built to get kerosene to the new site.

The lighthouse was taken out of service on June 16, 1933, and replaced by a lighted whistle buoy. The abandoned tower suffered vandalism, and later in the 1930s, a fire gutted the former keeper's house. The foundation of the old house was uncovered in 1995, and the best view of it is from the observation deck of the lighthouse.

Today the lighthouse serves as a landmark for those traveling the Intracoastal Waterway. It is accessible to the public, and visitors can explore the entire building by climbing its 176-step circular stairway to the top.

The former oil shed houses displays that relate the history of the lighthouse. A nonprofit group called Friends of Hunting Island State Park, along with the South Carolina State Park Service, is restoring the shed and the other outbuildings. These organizations hope to expand the on-site exhibits with more navigational aids and informational signs.

According to a plaque located between the lighthouse and the beach, "...between 1830 and 1875, over six tenths of a mile of Hunting Island's northern tip eroded away. The island lost another seven tenths of a mile to erosion by 1930. Hunting Island is eroding

COAST OF SOUTH CAROLINA.

ST. HELENA SOUND.

HUNTING ISLAND LIGHT STATION.
MAIN LIGHT REVOLVING, BEACON LIGHT FIXED.

Notice is hereby given that at sundown on Friday, the 1st day of July next, the new light-house and beacon on the north point of Hunting island, S. C., will be lighted, and will be kept burning during that night and every night thereafter from sunset to sunrise.

The main light-house is a conical tower built of reddish gray brick, the upper 25 feet of which will be colored white. The tower is surmounted by a brass lantern.

The illuminating apparatus is a lens of the second order of the system of Fresnel, showing a *revolving* light of the natural color, the interval between the flashes of which is 30 *seconds*. The tower is 95 feet high, and the focal plane is 108 feet above the level of the sea. The light should be visible in clear weather a distance of 17 nautical miles.

BEACON LIGHT.

The beacon light is on an open-work wooden frame, painted white, 32 feet high. The focal plane is 39 feet above the level of the sea. The illuminating apparatus is a lens of the sixth order of Fresnel; showing a *fixed* light of the natural color.

The direction of the range is N. 77° E. and S. 77° W. and the two lights and the outer buoy of the Slough or Northern channel are all in range. The bearings magnetic.

The position of the light as given by the Coast Survey is—

Latitude   32° 24' 30" N.
Longitude   80° 24' 30" W. of Greenwich.

The magnetic variation is 3° east.

After June 30 next the St. Helena bar light-vessel will be discontinued, and after she has been repaired she will be placed on Cambahee bank, St. Helena sound. Due notice of the time of placing her will be given.

By order of the Light-house Board :

W. H. C. WHITING,
Capt. Corps of Engrs., U. S. A.

SAVANNAH, GA.,
March 8, 1859.

an average annual rate of twenty-five feet on the northern tip and ten feet on the central beach."

Directions: The only South Carolina lighthouse that is open to the public is located sixteen miles south of Beaufort on US 21 in Hunting Island State Park. The park is connected to the mainland by an elevated highway across the marsh and Intracoastal Waterway (take US 17 to US 21). Follow signs to Hunting Island State Park, and take the second entrance to get to the lighthouse. There is a fee per car to enter the park and a nominal fee to tour the lighthouse. A knowledgeable attendant is available to lead tours or answer questions. There is also a nearby store that sells some convenience items and gifts.

Other Points of Interest

Historic Beaufort. This charming town and its historic homes can be seen by horse-drawn carriage, by car, or by a guided walking tour.

Bicycle Tours
843-812-4182

Boat Tours
843-671-5000

Carriage Tours
Carriage Tours of Beaufort, 843-521-1651
Carolina Buggy Tours, 843-525-1300
Mr. Ed's Carriage Tours, 843-522-3576

Van/Bus Tours
"The Point Historic Tours"
843-522-3576

Walking Tours
"The Spirit of Old Beaufort"
210 Scott's St.
843-525-0459

Useful Addresses and Resources

Greater Beaufort Chamber of Commerce
and
Beaufort Visitors Center
1006 Bay Street, Waterfront Park
PO Box 910
Beaufort, SC 29901
843-524-3163

Hunting Island State Park
2555 Sea Island Parkway
Hunting Island, SC 29920
843-838-2011

Open year-round, Hunting Island State Park is 5,000 acres of unspoiled marsh and beaches. It is a great place for camping, swimming, fishing and hiking. The park also has a 200-site camping area and fifteen rental cabins.

HILTON HEAD LIGHTHOUSE

Fast Facts

- The lighthouse was built in 1880 of steel, wood, and cast iron.
- It stands ninety-five feet tall.
- Hilton Head Lighthouse is one of only a handful of skeletal towers still in existence in America.

A group of West Indies landowners first sent English seaman William Hilton to explore Hilton Head Island in 1664. Partly to recognize the headlands that line Port Royal Sound and partly to honor Captain Hilton, the island got its name.

Almost two centuries later, in 1863 during the Civil War, a small tower was built with the help of Union soldiers who were stationed nearby. Not much is known about this original structure, which was destroyed by a storm only six years later.

After the war, Congress released $40,000 to purchase land and to put two range lights on Hilton Head Island. The lights were part of series of navigational aids, which included a lightship, to line Port Royal Sound. Because of a delay in obtaining land and clear title to it, the lighthouse wasn't built until 1880. It was finally illuminated in 1881.

The front beacon was a thirty-five foot tower atop the keeper's house, and the rear beacon was a separate ninety-five-foot tower. The front tower, separated from the rear by a distance of approximately one and a quarter miles, housed a flashing light almost six and a half feet in diameter. The rear beacon had a fixed white light measuring six feet in diameter. The two lights had to line up exactly, one above the other, so sea captains would know exactly how to enter the channel. Since the channel was always shifting, the front

Exterior view of rear Hilton Head Lighthouse, 1996. Terrance Zepke.

light was eventually made mobile in 1884 so the two lights could always be lined up.

There was also a second keeper's house, a boathouse, a small wharf, and several outbuildings, but all of these structures have been

Close-up of upper portion of beacon, 1996. Terrance Zepke.

destroyed by storms except for the rear beacon, the original keeper's quarters, and a brick oil shed. The former keeper's quarters were sold and moved, and currently house businesses at Harbour Town Marina.

The rear beacon, historically known as the Rear Lighthouse of Hilton Head Range Light Station, is now more commonly known as the Hilton Head Lighthouse. The tower is constructed of steel and

Brick oil shed, the only other structure remaining at site, 1996. Terrance Zepke.

Close-up of two of the six concrete foundations that anchor the tower, 1996. Each measures thirty feet in diameter. Terrance Zepke.

LIFE OF A LIGHTHOUSE KEEPER

Picture a lighthouse and its keeper—What do you think of? Halcyon days at the edge of the sea? Romantic, starlit evenings by the fire? The reality of this occupation was that it was often tedious, arduous, and desolate. Entries from a typical keeper's journal illustrate the loneliness and monotony of the lighthouse way of life.

January 11 - One barge passed at 8 P.M.
January 12 - Day of rest.
January 13 - Fixed and painted tank in storage shed.
January 14 - Filled and trimmed lamps.

Periodic inspections required that everything from the lighting apparatus to the "privy" be scrubbed, painted, and kept in top condition. Still, with all these responsibilities, pay was generally low. To better feed their families, most keepers on shore stations raised livestock and caught fish to supplement the staples they were allocated annually.

cast iron; the hexagonal-shaped watch room and lantern room are made of cypress. Six concrete foundation pilings, measuring thirty feet in diameter, securely anchor this massive structure to land. One of those concrete bases was put in the middle of the tower to support its 112-step circular metal staircase. The stairwell extends to the lantern, which is positioned 136 feet above sea level. In 1913, the wood that shingled the upper part of the rear beacon was replaced with steel sheathing.

The keeper carried kerosene, which was stored in the nearby oil shed, up the staircase several times a night, and then climbed the stairs again the following morning to put the lamp out. His days were spent cleaning the light and lantern room windows, trimming the wick, and getting ready for the evening's vigil.

A corps of United States Marines was stationed at the foot of the tower during World War II. Temporary barracks were constructed to house the troops, and a road leading to the beach was built. Several concrete pads were placed strategically along the beach to hold large anti-aircraft guns. An attack on these Marines never occurred, and the barracks and pads were removed after the war.

Hilton Head Lighthouse, 1940. Area was used then by U.S. Marine Corps to train defense battalions. Courtesy of Stephen R. Wise, curator of museum at Marine Corps Recruit Depot/Eastern Recruiting Region, Parris Island, SC.

Today, the structure is owned by Greenwood Development Corporation, which restored the tower in 1985 to highlight the Arthur Hills Golf Course at Palmetto Dunes Resort. The course is said to be one of the best on Hilton Head Island, and was specifically designed to include the lighthouse. Although the lighting sys-

First Hilton Head light tower, no date. Courtesy of National Archives.

tem was removed when the beacon was decommissioned in the 1930s, the whitewashed tower still has significant historical value. It is the only skeletal structure still in existence in the state, and is one of the few such structures remaining in the United States.

Directions: The lighthouse is located at the eighth hole of the Arthur Hills Golf Course at Palmetto Dunes Resort. Palmetto Dunes, located on Hilton Head Island and reached by US 278, is open only to members and their guests. The number for the resort is 843-785-1161.

NOTE: Due to the layout of the golf course and the large trees surrounding the lighthouse, it cannot be seen from any other vantage point.

Other Points of Interest

The Coastal Discovery Museum. The museum is a nonprofit environmental and historical organization that hosts various tours including Old House Plantation (former rice plantation), Pinckney Island Tours (wildlife, history, natural history, birding, etc., of National Wildlife

Close-up of Hilton Head Lighthouse, 1940. Courtesy of Stephen R. Wise, curator of museum at Marine Corps Recruit Depot/Eastern Recruiting Region, Parris Island, SC.

Refuge), Mitchelville and Fort Howell, beach tours, and much more. There's also a continuously running historical video, numerous displays, and a gift shop.

Coastal Discovery Museum. Housed in the same facility as the Hilton Head Island Chamber of Commerce Welcome Center

100 William Hilton Parkway
Hilton Head Island, SC 29925
843-689-6767

Historic Savannah, Georgia. This city is about 45 miles south of Hilton Head Island and also offers many great activities for tourists.

Sightseeing Tour Companies of Savannah

Old Savannah Tours
1-800-517-9007

Old Town Trolley Tours
912-233-0083

Gray Line Tours
912-234-8687

River Street Riverboat Co.
800-786-6404

Or check out one of Georgia's best lighthouses:

Tybee Island Lighthouse and Museum
Tybee Island, Georgia
912-786-5801

Useful Addresses and Resources

Hilton Head Central Reservations
1-800-845-7018
The resource for all island accommodations, including hotels, condominiums, villas, and houses. Also provides golf packages, since Hilton Head is a golfer's paradise and acts as host to the PGA tour's MCI Classic Golf Tournament.

Hilton Head Island Chamber of Commerce Welcome Center
100 William Hilton Parkway
Hilton Head Island, SC 29925
843-689-6767
Visit the Welcome Center for brochures on accommodations, restaurants, and activities, and for maps and directions to anywhere on the island.

Hilton Head Chamber of Commerce
One Chamber Drive
Hilton Head Island, SC 29925
843-785-3673

Savannah Area Convention & Visitors Bureau
P.O. Box 1628
222 W. Oglethorpe Ave., Suite 100
Savannah, GA 31402-1628
912-944-0456
Located in a restored Georgia railroad station, the Convention & Visitors Bureau offers visitor guides and information on Savannah's historic district. The 1860s building also houses a history museum. Within walking distance is the Ships of the Sea Museum, featuring an extensive collection of maritime models and memorabilia.

HARBOUR TOWN LIGHTHOUSE

Fast Facts

- The lighthouse is a symbol of the Harbour Town Marina on Hilton Head Island.
- The ninety-foot-high lighthouse was completed in 1970.
- Although it's mostly decorative, it is a functioning lighthouse.

Harbour Town Lighthouse was the last tower built—and the first one privately financed since 1817—in South Carolina. Construction on the $68,000 tower began in 1969 and was completed the following year. The hexagonal-shaped beacon is an elaborate structure designed to minimize maintenance by protecting it from salt water and corrosion. Its exterior is composed of several layers: the visible, top layer is stucco, which is attached to a metal lath. The lath is attached to one-inch by three-inch wood furring strips, which in turn are attached to three-quarter-inch plywood sheathing. Lastly, the sheathing is attached to three-inch by four-inch treated wood walers (sic).

Anchored by a heavy concrete base, the little red-and-white-striped tower stands ninety feet tall and has 110 stairs leading up to its blinking light. The beacon flashes every two and a half seconds from a low-watt bulb, which can be seen by boaters fifteen miles away on a clear night.

While it does serve as a navigational aid for boats coming into Harbour Town Marina, its main purpose is as a symbol of Sea Pines Plantation. Sea Pines is a residential and commercial development located on Hilton Head Island, facing the Calibogue Sound and Intracoastal Waterway.

The beacon is open to the public daily. Plaques illustrating the history of Harbour Town and the lighthouse line the tower's interior

Plaque inside Harbour Town Lighthouse that shows before and after photos of the lighthouse's construction, 1996. Terrance Zepke.

Tower observation deck and rooftop, 1996. Terrance Zepke.

walls. A gift shop is located at the top of the tower, in addition to an observation area that rewards climbers with a great view of the island and the sound.

NOTE: Some lighthouse experts and enthusiasts argue this structure doesn't merit mention in a legitimate book on lighthouses, since it is mostly decorative. I chose to include it because it is a functioning lighthouse listed on Coast Guard maps.

Directions: Take US 278 to Hilton Head Island. Follow signs into Sea Pines Plantation. At the entrance there is a security gate where visitors, at little cost, may purchase a day pass. Proceed by taking Greenwood Drive to Lighthouse Road and on to Harbour Town.

Harbour Town Lighthouse as seen from marina, 1996. Terrance Zepke.

There is ample parking at the marina, and surrounding the tower are numerous shops and eating establishments. Admission to the lighthouse itself is free.

Other Points of Interest

The Coastal Discovery Museum. The museum is a nonprofit environmental and historical organization that hosts various tours including Old House Plantation (former rice plantation), Pinckney Island Tours (wildlife, history, natural history, birding, etc., of National Wildlife Refuge), Mitchelville and Fort Howell, beach tours, and much more. There's also a continuously running historical video, numerous displays, and a gift shop.

Coastal Discovery Museum
Housed in the same facility as the Hilton Head Island Chamber of Commerce Welcome Center
100 William Hilton Parkway
Hilton Head Island, SC 29925
843-689-6767

The Harbour Town Lighthouse began construction in 1969 and was completed in the Spring of 1970. Some who thought it senseless to build such a structure in an effort to attract boaters along the Intracoastal Waterway, called it "Fraser's Folly."

Avron B. Fogelman purchased the Harbour Town area in 1987 to protect and enhance the quality lifestyle first envisioned by Charles Fraser and dedicated on June 17, 1989, with Mr. Fraser's other friends, this famous neck of land as Fraser Point, in recognition of Charles E. Fraser's vision, leadership and creativity.

However, within a decade, Fraser's Folly became acclaimed as a "stroke of genius." Strategically situated not only for yachtsmen, but for network television cameras looking down the 18th fairway of the Harbour Town Golf links during the Heritage Golf Classic, the red-and-white striped lighthouse had become the symbol for all of Hilton Head Island as well as South Carolina. It is now recognized as one of the nation's best known landmarks.

The Fraser of the lighthouse was Charles E. Fraser, founder of Sea Pines Plantation and several other destination-resort communities launched in the 1960's and since revolutionizing the standards of resort development worldwide.

Plaque inside Harbour Town Lighthouse that explains the premise behind its construction, 1996. Terrance Zepke.

Historic Savannah, Georgia. This city is about 45 miles south of Hilton Head Island and also offers many great activities for tourists.

Sightseeing Tour Companies of Savannah

Old Savannah Tours
1-800-517-9007

Old Town Trolley Tours
912-233-0083

Gray Line Tours
912-234-8687

River Street Riverboat Co.
800-786-6404

Or check out one of Georgia's best lighthouses:

Tybee Island Lighthouse and Museum
Tybee Island, Georgia
912-786-5801

Useful Addresses and Resources

Hilton Head Central Reservations
1-800-845-7018
The resource for all island accommodations, including hotels, condominiums, villas, and houses. Also provides golf packages, since Hilton Head is a golfer's paradise, and acts as host to the MCI and Heritage Gold Golf tournaments.

Hilton Head Island Chamber of Commerce Welcome Center
100 William Hilton Parkway
Hilton Head Island, SC 29925
843-689-6767

Visit the Welcome Center for brochures on accommodations, restaurants, and activities, and for maps and directions to anywhere on the island.

Hilton Head Chamber of Commerce
One Chamber Drive
Hilton Head Island, SC 29925
843-785-3673

Savannah Area Convention & Visitors Bureau
P.O. Box 1628
222 W. Oglethorpe Ave., Suite 100
Savannah, GA 31402-1628
912-944-0456

Located in a restored Georgia railroad station, the Convention & Visitors Bureau offers visitor guides and information on Savannah's historic district. The 1860s building also houses a history museum. Within walking distance is the Ships of the Sea Museum, featuring an extensive collection of maritime models and memorabilia.

HAIG POINT LIGHTHOUSE AND BLOODY POINT LIGHTHOUSE

Fast Facts

- One owner of Bloody Point Lighthouse, Arthur Burn, considered Daufuskie Island "the nearest place to heaven as one could get on earth."
- The first of Haig Point's three keepers was Patrick Comer, whose salary was $560 a year; his wife Bridget was the assistant keeper, and she earned $400 a year.

In May of 1872, five acres on Daufuskie Island was sold for $745 to the federal government. That same year the government released $15,000 to put "two sets of range lights on or near Daufuskie Island." Four lights—the first pair at Haig Point and the other at Bloody Point—were constructed on Daufuskie Island by October 1873. The lights guided vessels to the ports of Savannah and Charleston from the Atlantic Ocean through Calibogue Sound and the Intracoastal Waterway.

The lights located at the northern end of the island were named after wealthy plantation owner George Haig. The two lights were approximately one-half mile from one another. The rear light was a wooden tower, positioned on top of the keeper's house, seventy feet above sea level. A 5th-order Fresnel lens contained a fixed white light which was fueled by lamp oil. A fence surrounding this immobile beacon was added in 1879 to keep the island's roaming cattle away from the house and outbuildings.

The front beacon was seventeen feet above sea level. It was also made of wood, and it housed a steamer lens (originally made

Front beacon light of Haig Point (located a half mile from rear beacon and moved by oxen whenever channel shifted), 1885. Courtesy of National Archives.

for steam engine locomotives) rather than a Fresnel lens. Since the channel frequently changed, the front beacon could be moved so the lights would always line up.

In 1925, the Haig Point Lighthouse and accompanying land were sold for about $1500 to M.V. Haas, who turned the property into a hunting retreat. Grand parties were held at the site until a

Rear beacon light of Haig Point, 1885. Courtesy of National Archives.

drunken guest climbed to the top of the lighthouse one night and accidentally plummeted to his death. Subsequent owners attempted to restore the property, which slowly fell into a state of disrepair, but it wasn't until International Paper Realty Corporation bought the site in 1984 that any real restoration work began.

The Haig Point restoration team kept to the original floor plans as much as possible using microfilm found at the Coast Guard Academy. This microfilm shows the original plans and even includes alterations done to the lighthouse between 1870 and 1912. During these renovations, led by well-known restoration architect William Phillips, the team discovered that the rear Haig Point Lighthouse had

Haig Point during its deterioration, 1963. Courtesy of Savannah newspaper.

been built on the foundation of an 1838 house. This foundation has been preserved.

The team installed an acrylic "window" in the kitchen floor of the Haig Point Lighthouse to showcase the large fireplace of the 1838 plantation house. They also discovered that the bricks at the base of the lighthouse came from a mansion that had been built by William "Squire" Pope, a well-to-do businessman and

Haig Point dining room, highlighting fireplace, 1997. Photo by Matthew Gardiner. Courtesy of International Paper Realty Corporation.

landowner from Hilton Head. The mansion was destroyed during the Civil War.

Restorations to the lighthouse were completed in April 1986. On October 17, 1986, the Victorian structure was recommissioned during a gala hosted by International Paper Realty Corporation. The festivities included performances by the Savannah Symphony and a Marine Corps Color Guard. A picnic and fireworks display completed the celebration.

Today, the former Haig Point keeper's dwelling is used by International Paper as a guest house. In addition to the kitchen annex, there are two upstairs bedrooms, a parlor, and a dining room. Great care has been taken to furnish the house with period antiques. Even the former cistern and oil house have been cleaned and are in good condition.

Although the lights at Haig Point were officially discontinued in July 1924, today the rear light is listed on Coast Guard maps as a private aid to navigation. Its lantern room, reached through a series of ladders and stairs, houses a 247-candlepower beam encased in a large acrylic optic lens. The light, visible from over nine and a half miles away, is powered by a solar battery. Its flash pattern is two seconds on and ten seconds off.

Bloody Point Lighthouse. Courtesy of Melrose Corporation.

On the southeastern tip of Daufuskie Island were the two Bloody Point range lights. (Bloody Point was named after two massacres, known as the Yemasee Indian War of 1715, that took place on this part of the island.) The lights were almost identical to those at Haig Point: the rear light was a fixed tower on the keeper's house; the front, a moveable beacon. The white, two-story keeper's house had two large rooms downstairs, two bedrooms upstairs, and both front and back porches.

In 1922, Bloody Point Light was shut down by its last keeper, Arthur Ashley Burn. Following the beacon's decommission, the tower was removed from the house. The lights and five acres of land were sold at public auction.

Haig Point and foundation outline of former plantation home discovered during restoration, 1994. Photo by Paul Barton. Courtesy of International Paper Realty Corporation.

Like Haig Point, Bloody Point has had several owners, and by the early 1980s it too was in poor shape. Its new owner, Melrose Corporation, repaired the rear beacon's foundation and porches, and replaced missing windows and panes. The downstairs was made into one large room, and a new staircase was built. A bathroom was added upstairs, and the house was painted red with white trim. Other renovations were done earlier when the keeper's house served briefly as the Daufuskie Lighthouse Inn. The keeper's house is now a pro shop.

Directions: Haig Point Lighthouse is privately owned and not open to visitors. It can be seen from Hilton Head Island's Harbour Town, or from a boat on Calibogue Sound. A public boat dock is available on Daufuskie, and boats can be rented or launched from Savannah, Harbour Town, or elsewhere on Hilton Head Island. The only vehicles allowed at Haig Point are bicycles, horse-drawn buggies, and golf carts.

Bloody Point Lighthouse is part of the Daufuskie Golf Club and is accessible only to members and guests.

Other Points of Interest

Daufuskie Island. The island has several historic sites, and the nearby areas of Savannah, Georgia and Hilton Head Island, South Carolina offer great seafood, shopping, historical walking tours, and boat outings.

The Coastal Discovery Museum. The museum is a nonprofit environmental and historical organization that hosts various tours including Old House Plantation (former rice plantation), Pinckney Island Tours (wildlife, history, natural history, birding, etc., of National Wildlife Refuge), Mitchelville and Fort Howell, beach tours, and much more. There's also a continuously running historical video, numerous displays, and a gift shop.

Coastal Discovery Museum
Housed in the same facility as the Hilton Head Island Chamber of Commerce Welcome Center
100 William Hilton Parkway
Hilton Head Island, SC 29925
843-689-6767

Or check out one of Georgia's best lighthouses:

Tybee Island Lighthouse and Museum
Tybee Island, Georgia
912-786-5801

Useful Addresses and Resources

Hilton Head Central Reservations
1-800-845-7018
The resource for all island accommodations, including hotels, condominiums, villas, and houses. Also provides golf packages, since Hilton Head is a golfer's paradise, and acts as host to the PGA tour's MCI Classic Golf Tournament.

Hilton Head Island Chamber of Commerce Welcome Center
100 William Hilton Parkway
Hilton Head Island, SC 29925
843-689-6767

Visit the Welcome Center for brochures on accommodations, restaurants, and activities, and for maps and directions to anywhere on the island.

Hilton Head Chamber of Commerce
One Chamber Drive
Hilton Head Island, SC 29925
843-785-3673

Savannah Area Convention & Visitors Bureau
P.O. Box 1628
222 W. Oglethorpe Ave., Suite 100
Savannah, GA 31402-1628
912-944-0456

Located in a restored Georgia railroad station, the Convention & Visitors Bureau offers visitor guides and information on Savannah's historic district. The 1860s building also houses a history museum. Within walking distance is the Ships of the Sea Museum, featuring an extensive collection of maritime models and memorabilia.

Sightseeing Tour Companies of Savannah

Old Savannah Tours
1-800-517-9007

Old Town Trolley Tours
912-233-0083

Gray Line Tours
912-234-8687

River Street Riverboat Co.
800-786-6404

LIGHTHOUSE ORGANIZATIONS AND RESOURCES

Lighthouse Digest
Box 1690
Wells, Maine 04090
1-800-758-1444
Lighthouse Digest is a monthly periodical full of lighthouse information and a catalog of current nautical products available.

Lighthouse Gifts
1-1/2 miles north of Rt. 109 junction
U.S. 1
Wells, Maine 04090
1-207-646-0608
A lighthouse gift store and producer of catalog called *Lighthouse Depot*, offering lighthouse memorabilia.

NC Chamber of Commerce
GRCC
P.O. Box 2978
Raleigh, NC 27602
1-919-664-7000

NC Ferry Information
1-800-BYFERRY (293-3779)

NC Travel & Tourism Division
Department of Commerce
430 N. Salisbury St.
Raleigh, NC 27611
1-919-733-4171

Outer Banks History Center
P.O. Box 250
Highway 400
Ice Plant Island
Manteo, NC 27954
252-473-2655
A great source of lighthouse photographs, diagrams, and Outer Banks maritime history.

Outer Banks Lighthouse Society
210 Gallery Row
Nags Head, NC 27959
252-441-4232
A nonprofit organization (affiliated with Lighthouse Gallery) dedicated to preserving the Outer Banks sentinels. Quarterly newsletter and invitations to special events are included as part of the annual membership dues.

SC State Chamber of Commerce
1201 Main St.
Suite 1810
Columbia, SC 29201
1-803-799-4601

SC Parks Department
Recreation & Tourism
P.O. Box 71
Columbia, SC 29201-0071
1-800-962-6262

SC Travel & Tourism Bureau
1205 Pendleton St.
Suite 110
Edger Brown Building
Columbia, SC 29201
1-803-751-6219

U.S. Lighthouse Society
244 Kearny St., 5th floor
San Francisco, CA 94108
415-362-7255

A 5,000 member organization founded to preserve and promote lighthouses through various programs and tours. The society produces a newsletter and catalog, which includes lighthouse products. Annual membership dues.

INDEX

Numbers in **bold** indicate pages where photos or illustrations may be found. "C" page numbers indicate color insert pages.

lightering pilots, 39
Lighthouse Board, xii, 5, 50, 77, 79, 105, 127
Lighthouse Club, 10
Lighthouse Inlet, 115
Lighthouse Island, 103, 107, **109**, 110
Lookout Shoals, 49
Louisiana, 89

M

malaria, 24, 129
Marine Corps, 72, 141, **142**
Marine Corps Color Guard, 157
Marine Corps Recuit Depot, **142**, **144**
Massachusetts, 35, 45
Maynard, Robert, 41
McClellanville, 109, 110
MCI Classic Golf Tournament, 145, 152, 161
Melrose Corporation, 158, **158**
Middle Bay, 113-114
Miller, Adam, 113
Mitchelville, 144, 150, 160
Morehead City, 47, 53-55
Morris Island, xi, 113, 115, 117, 118, **118**, 119
Morris Island Lighthouse, 113, **115**, 118, 121, **C2**
Morrison, 113
Morrison Island, 115
mosquito farm, **27**
Mt. Pleasant, 111, 119, 124
murder, 105
museum, 9-11, 32, 50, 54, 84, 120, 125, 143, 146, 152, 161
Myrtle Beach, 84

N

Nags Head, 13, 19, 33
National Archives, **4**, **64**, **65**, 68, 98, **99**, **109**, **114**, 115, **115**, **116**, **117**, **124**, **125**, **143**, **154**, **155**
National Maritime Initiative, 115, 121
National Park Service, xii, **14**, 18, 26, **26**, 27, **27**, 32, 47, 48, 52, **133**
National Register of Historic Places, 9, 47-48, 50, 54, 86, 124
Navy, United States, 83, 98
New Inlet, 57, 63, 77
North Carolina, xi, xii, xiii, 1, 9, 18, 21, 32, 35, 39, 41, 49, 54, 57, 68, 75, 116
North Carolina Coastal Resources Management Commission, 32
North Carolina General Assembly, 42
North Carolina Maritime Museum, 54
North Carolina State Archives, **5**, **6**, **15**, **16**, **22**, **23**, **24**, 25, **28**, **36**, **43**, **45**, **46**, **51**, **53**, **60**, **61**, **65**, **66**, 77, 78, **79**, **80**, **82**, **85**, **90**, **92**, **104**, **106**, **107**, **116**
North Carolina State University, 31
North Carolina Travel and Tourism, **51**, **C2**, **C5**
North Island, 97, 100
Norway, 105
Notice to Mariners, 127, **133**

If you enjoyed reading this book, here are some other books from Pineapple Press on related topics. For a complete catalog, write to: Pineapple Press, P.O. Box 3899, Sarasota, FL 34230 or call 1-800-PINEAPL (746-3275).

The Florida Keys: A History of the Pioneers by John Viele. As vividly portrayed as if they were characters in a novel, the true-life inhabitants of the Florida Keys will capture your admiration as you share in the dreams and realities of their daily lives.
ISBN: 1-56164-101-4 (HB)

Guardians of the Lights by Elinor De Wire. Stories of the men and women of the U.S. Lighthouse Service. In a charming blend of history and human interest, this book paints a colorful portrait of the lives of a vanished breed.
ISBN: 1-56164-077-8 (HB); 1-56164-119-7 (PB)

Guide to Florida Lighthouses by Elinor De Wire. Its lighthouses are some of Florida's oldest and most historic structures, with diverse styles of architecture and daymark designs.
ISBN: 0-910923-74-4 (PB)

Key Biscayne: A History of Miami's Tropical Island and the Cape Florida Lighthouse by Joan Gill Blank. This is the engaging biography of the southernmost barrier island in the United States and the Cape Florida Lighthouse that has stood at its southern tip for 170 years.
ISBN: 1-56164-096-4 (HB); 1-56164-103-0 (PB)

Legendary Islands of the Ocean Sea by Robert H. Fuson. From the diaries and charts of early explorers comes the intriguing story of the real and imagined islands of what we now know as the Atlantic and Pacific Oceans.
ISBN: 1-56164-078-6 (HB)

Lighthouses of Ireland by Kevin M. McCarthy with paintings by William L. Trotter. Eighty navigational aids under the authority of the Commissioners of Irish Lights dot the two thousand miles of Irish coastline. Each is addressed here, and thirty of the most interesting ones are featured with detailed histories and full-color paintings.
ISBN: 1-56164-131-6 (HB)

Lighthouses of the Florida Keys by Love Dean. In this historical account, you'll visit the lights throughout the Florida Keys — ones that once existed and the ones still standing today — and meet the many keepers who tended them. You'll also learn the history of the individ-

ual lights, including construction, repairs needed due to storms, and the politics which have always swirled around them.
ISBN: 1-56164-160-X (HB); 1-56164-165-0 (PB)

Search for the Great Turtle by Jack Rudloe with illustrations by Marty Capron. Intrigued by turtle legends from many cultures, Rudloe travels the globe observing the silent rituals of sea turtles and learns timeless lessons about conservation and respect for the earth.
ISBN: 1-56164-072-7 (HB)

Shipwrecks of Florida: A Comprehensive Listing (second edition) by Steven D. Singer. This thoroughly updated edition includes general information on research, search and salvage, wreck identification, arti-fact conservation, and rights to wrecks, which accompanies a listing of over 2,100 wrecks off the Florida coast from the sixteenth century to the present.
ISBN: 1-56164-163-4 (PB)

The Spanish Treasure Fleets by Timothy R. Walton. The story of how the struggle to control precious metals from Spain's colonies in Latin America helped to shape the modern world.
ISBN: 1-56164-049-2 (HB)

Thirty Florida Shipwrecks by Kevin M. McCarthy with paintings by William L. Trotter. Sunken treasure, prison ships, Nazi submarines, and the Bermuda triangle make what the Florida Historical Quarterly calls "exciting history."
ISBN: 1-56164-007-7 (PB)

Twenty Florida Pirates by Kevin M. McCarthy with paintings by William L. Trotter. Notorious Florida pirates from the 1500s to the pre-sent include Sir Francis Drake, Black Caesar, Blackbeard, and José Gaspar — not to mention present-day drug smugglers.
ISBN: 1-56164-050-6 (PB)

Also be sure to check out Terrance Zepke's latest book, slated for pub-lication in 1999: *Ghosts of the Carolina Coasts: Ghosts of the Carolinas' Lighthouses, Plantations, and Other Historic Sites.* It offers numerous spine-tingling tales that have sprung straight from low-country oral tradition.

LIGHTHOUSES OF THE CAROLINAS

A Short History and Guide